THE
AMERICAN CONSTITUTIONS
AND RELIGION

Religious References in the
Charters of the Thirteen Colonies
and the
Constitutions of the Forty-eight States

A Source-book on
Church and State in the United States

Compiled by
CONRAD HENRY MOEHLMAN
James B. Colgate Professor of the
History of Christianity at The Colgate-
Rochester Divinity School

Berne, Indiana
1938

To

Shirley Jackson Case

whose accurate interpretation of the sources of
The History of Christianity
has made all co-workers his debtors.

Books by the same author:

Theos Soter as Title and Name of Jesus

The Unknown Bible

The Story of the Ten Commandments

The Catholic-Protestant Mind

The Story of Christianity in Outline

The Christian-Jewish Tragedy

TABLE OF CONTENTS

CONTENTS 7

8 CONTENTS

CONTENTS

Page

CONTENTS

10

INTRODUCTORY

The history of church-state relations in the area of the United States is clearly divisible into five periods with the sixth period recently emerging. The cuts are made at 1776, 1791, 1837, 1876, and 1930.

During the long colonial period ending with the Declaration of Independence in 1776, the settlers from England and Europe were adjusting themselves to the new conditions of life in the western hemisphere. Their thinking was largely of the English-European pattern. The new political and religious ideas of the sixteenth and seventeenth centuries were being imported to America. The toleration enunciated in the settlement of Westphalia, 1648, and in the much more important English Act of Toleration, 1689, was somewhat realized in the new land. To the outbreak of the Revolutionary War, Roman Catholics were not in great favor and their number and social standing not of the kind to enable the Catholic church to play a determining role in the development of American religious life. More than ninety-nine per cent. of the population in the area of the United States was non-Catholic. Of the 22,000 Roman Catholics in the population, some 15,000 were living in Maryland. The majority of the remainder dwelt in Pennsylvania, with Philadelphia as the American Catholic metropolis.

New England with the exception of dissenters in Rhode Island was solidly Congregational. Moreover the Baptists were using the Westminster and Savoy faith summaries, making them Congregational except in the matters of baptism and possibly religious freedom. The South was Anglican, although its Anglicanism was of a loose texture. In the Middle Colonies, religious syncretism was on. Here Anglicans, Congregationalists, Reformed, Lutherans, Baptists, Presbyterians, Friends, Mennonites, Moravians, and toward the very end of the colonial period Methodists and Shakers were rubbing against each other all the time and especially during revival movements.

The second period in the history of church-state relations in the United States began with the Virginia Declaration of

Rights in 1776 and ended with the adoption of the first ten amendments to the constitution of the United States in 1791. This decade and one-half is fundamental in the development of the American doctrine of separation of church and state. Where in the colonial period religious liberty is proposed, the argument runs along divine right lines. Now religious liberty becomes a natural right. It was on July 2, 1777 that a convention meeting at Windsor framed a constitution for Vermont whose third section of Chapter I began: "That all men have a natural and unalienable right to worship Almighty God, according to the dictates of their own consciences and understanding, regulated by the word of God . . ."

Pennsylvania and North Carolina had so declared in 1776.

The first constitution of Virginia, 1776, began: "We, the Delegates and Representatives of the good people of Virginia, do declare the future form of government of Virginia to be as followeth . . ." To one who has observed the numerous references to God and Bible in the colonial charters and laws, the complete omission of reference to God and Christianity is exceedingly impressive.

Another epoch-making declaration is encountered in the Virginia Act for establishing religious freedom, 1786, in which toward the end it is stated that religious rights "are of *the natural rights of mankind,* and that if any act shall hereafter be passed to repeal the present, or to narrow its operation, *such act will be an infringement of natural right.*"

The importance of the Vermont and Virginia definition of religious liberty as a natural right may be observed by recalling that of the twelve states admitted into the American union between Kentucky and Michigan, eight use the phrase "natural and indefeasible right" of religious liberty and three others affirm the principle of religious liberty in other words. Only Louisiana remains silent in this early period in regard to the matter.

Article VI, Section 3 of the Constitution of the United States reads: "but no religious test shall ever be required as a qualification to any office or public trust under the United States," while the First Amendment contains: "Congress shall make no law respecting an establishment of religion, or prohibiting the free exercise thereof"—thus guaranteeing religious liberty as far as the nation was concerned. But the religious arrangements in the thirteen original states were not affected thereby.

On July 13, 1787, Congress arranged for the government of the territory of the United States northwest of the River Ohio stating that "no person, demeaning himself in a peaceable and orderly manner, shall ever be molested on account of his mode of worship or religious sentiments in the said territory."

In the third period in the history of church-state relations in the the United States, 1791-1837, the original constitutions of all states admitted to the Union with the exception of Louisiana contain very definite avowals of religious liberty.

Various Protestant confessions of Faith are modified or rewritten to conform to the free church in a free state principle. Roman Catholicism is also characterized, 1829-1852, by "native Americanism." Trustees of prominent Roman Catholic churches here and there, influenced by the vigorous democratic movement all about them, claimed the right to nominate and elect and confer jurisdiction upon their priests. Occasionally they resisted the decisions of the pope "as of foreign jurisdiction" and Bishop Carroll led the movement which secured to the "American hierarchy the right of recommending suitable persons for vacancies in the episcopate." In 1826, Bishop England even addressed the Congress of the United States. His stirring defense of the Constitution of the United States contained: "Let the Pope and the Cardinals and all the powers of the Catholic world united make the least encroachment on that Constitution, we will protest it with our lives. Summon a General Council—let that Council interfere in the mode of our electing but an assistant to a turnkey of a prison—we deny the right, we reject the usurpation."

During this third period, the relation of public education to the church began to be discussed. Here Virginia again led the way. As early as 1818, the commissioners appointed to fix the site of the University of Virginia reported:

"Indeed we need look back half a century, to times which many now living remember well, and see the wonderful advances in the sciences and arts which have been made within that period. Some of these have rendered the elements themselves subservient to the purposes of man, have harnessed them to the yoke of his labors, and effected the great blessings of moderating his own, of accomplishing what was beyond his feeble force, and extending the comforts of life to a much enlarged circle, to those who had before known its necessaries only. That these are not the vain dreams of sanguine hope, we have before our eyes real and living examples. What, but education, has advanced us beyond the condition of our indigenous neighbors? And what chains them to their present state of barbarism and wretchedness, but a bigotted veneration for the supposed superlative wisdom of their fathers, and the preposterous idea that they are to look backward for better things, and not forward, longing, as it should seem, to return to the days of eating acorns and roots, rather than indulge in the degeneracies of civilization? And how much more encouraging to the achievements of science and improvement is this, than the desponding view that the condition of man cannot be ameliorated, that what has been must ever be, and that to secure ourselves where we are, we must tread with awful reverence in the footsteps of our fathers. This doctrine is the genuine fruit of the alliance between Church and State; the tenants of which, finding themselves but too well in their present condition, oppose all advances which might unmask their usurpations, and monopolies of honors, wealth, and power, and fear every change, as endangering the comforts they now hold."

"In conformity with the principles of our Constitution, which places all sects of religion on an equal footing, with the jealousies of the different sects in guarding that equality from encroachment and surprise, and with the sentiments of the Legislature in favor of freedom of religion, manifested on former occasions, we have proposed no professor of divinity; and the rather as the proofs of the being of a God, the creator, preserver, and supreme ruler of the universe, the author of all the relations of morality, and of the laws and obligations these infer, will be within the province of the professor of ethics; to which adding the developments of these moral obligations, of those in which all sects agree, with a knowledge of the languages, Hebrew, Greek, and Latin, a basis will be formed common to all sects. Proceeding thus far without offence to the Constitution, we have thought it proper at this point to leave every sect to provide, as they think fittest, the means of further instruction in their own peculiar tenets."

Again in 1819, Thomas Jefferson wrote:

"In our University you know there is no Professorship of Divinity. A handle has been made of this, to disseminate an idea that this is an institution, not merely of no religion, but against all religion. . . . In our annual report to the legislature, after stating the constitutional reasons against a public establishment of any religious instruction, we suggest the expediency of encouraging the different religious sects to establish, each for itself, a professorship of their own tenets, on the confines of the university, so near as that their students may attend lectures there, and have the free use of our library, and every other accommodation we can give them; preserving, however, their independence of us and each other. This fills the chasm objected to in ours, as a defect in an institution professing to give instruction in all useful sciences. I think the invitation will be accepted, by some sects from candid intentions, and by others from jealousy and rivalship. And by bringing the sects together, we shall soften their asperities, liberalize and neutralize their prejudices, and make the general religion a religion of peace, reason, and morality."

In the fourth period in the relations between state and church in the United States, 1837-1876, the constitutions of the states joining the union generously recognize the principle of religious liberty. The principal issue is the question of the emancipation of public education from ecclesiastical control. Horace Mann as secretary of the Massachusetts State Board of Education, in a series of twelve reports, 1837-1848, did pioneer missionary work in behalf of the independent rights of public education.

The following autobiographical narrative indicates the type of religion to which Horace Mann was reacting:

"Like all children, I believed what I was taught. To my vivid imagination, a physical hell was a living reality, as much so as though I could have heard the shrieks of the tormented, or stretched out my hand to grasp their burning souls, in a vain endeavor for their rescue. Such a faith spread a pall of blackness over the whole heavens, shutting out every beautiful and glorious thing; while beyond that curtain of darkness I could see the bottomless and seething lake filled with torments, and hear the wailing and agony of its victims. . . . Had there been any possibility of escape, could penance, fasting, self-inflicted wounds, or the pains of a thousand martyr-deaths, have averted the fate, my agony of apprehension would have been alleviated; but there, beyond effort, beyond virtue, beyond hope, was this irreversible decree of Jehovah, immutable, from everlasting. . . . The consequences upon my mind and happiness were disastrous in the extreme. Often, on going to bed at night, did the objects of the day and the faces of friends give place to a vision of the awful throne, the inexorable judge, and the hapless myriads, among whom I often seemed to see those whom I loved best; and there I wept and sobbed until Nature found that counterfeit repose in exhaustion whose genuine reality she should have found in freedom from care and spontaneous happiness of childhood."

The following excerpt from the chapter *Deception* in Abbott's *Child at Home* indicates what children were being taught:

"But we must not forget that there is a day of most solemn judgment near at hand. When you die, your body will be wrapped in the shroud, and placed in the coffin and buried in the grave; and there it will remain and moulder to the dust, while the snows of unnumbered winters, and the tempests of unnumbered summers, shall rest upon the cold earth which covers you. But your spirit will not be there. Far away, beyond the cloudless skies, and blazing suns, and twinkling stars, it will have gone to judgment. How awful must be the scene which will open before you, as you enter the eternal world! You will see the throne of God: how bright, how glorious, will it burst upon your sight! You will see God the Savior seated upon that majestic throne. Angels, in numbers more than can be counted, will fill the universe with their glittering wings, and their rapturous songs. Oh, what a scene to behold! And then you will stand in the presence of this countless throng to answer for every thing you have done while you lived. Every action and every thought of your life will then be fresh in your mind. You know it is written in the Bible, "God will bring every work into judgment, with every secret thing, whether it be good or whether it be evil." How must the child then feel who has been guilty of falsehood and deception, and has it then all brought to light! No liar can enter the kingdom of heaven. Oh, how dreadful must be the confusion and shame with which the deceitful child will then be overwhelmed! The angels will all see your sin and your disgrace. And do you think they will wish to have a liar enter heaven, to be associated with them? No! They must turn from you with disgust. The Savior will look upon you in his displeasure. Conscience will rend your soul. And you must hear the awful sentence, "Depart from me, into everlasting fire, prepared for the devil and his angels." Oh, it is a dreadful thing to practice deceit. It will shut you from heaven. It will confine you in eternal woe. Though you should escape detection as long as you live; though you should die, and your falsehood not be discovered, the time will soon come when it will all be brought to light, and when the whole universe of men and of angels will be witnesses of your shame. If any child who reads this feels condemned for past deceptions, oh, beware, and do not postpone repentance till the day of judgment shall arrive."

The fifth period in the relations between church and state in the United States was ushered in by President Grant's address to the army of the Tennessee on September 29, 1875, at Des Moines, Iowa, in which he advocated a public school system separated from ecclesiastical control:

"Let us then begin by guarding against every enemy threatening this perpetuity of free republican institutions. . . . *The free school is the promoter of that intelligence which is to preserve us.* . . . If we are to have another contest in the near future of our national existence I predict that the dividing line will not be Mason and Dixon's but between patriotism and intelligence on the one side and superstition, ambition, and ignorance on the other. The centennial year of our national existence, I believe, is a good time to begin the work of strengthening the foundations of the structure commenced by our patriotic forefathers 100 years ago at Lexington. Let us all labor to add all needful guarantees for the security of free thought, free speech, a free press, pure morals, *unfettered religious sentiments,* and of equal rights and privileges to all men, irrespective of nationality, color, or religion. *Encourage free schools and resolve that not one dollar appropriated for their support shall be appropriated to the support of any sectarian schools.* Resolve that either the state or the nation, or both combined, shall support institutions of learning sufficient to afford to every child growing up in the land the opportunity of a good common school education, unmixed with sectarian, pagan, or atheistical dogmas. *Leave the matter of religion to the family circle, the church, and the private school supported entirely by private contributions. Keep the church and state forever separate.*"

In his next message to Congress, President Grant recommended an amendment to the Constitution of the United States forbidding teaching in any public school of religious tenets and prohibiting the granting of school funds or taxes for any religious sect or denomination.

The Blaine Amendment incorporating these emphases was passed by the House on August 4, 1876. In the Senate, the amendment could not muster the necessary two-thirds vote, although all the Republicans voted for it.

The revised Blaine Constitutional Amendment submitted to the Senate on August 14, 1876, read:

"No State shall make any law respecting an establishment of religion or prohibiting the free exercise thereof; and no religious test shall ever be required as a qualification to any office or public trust under any State. No public property, and no public revenue of, nor any loan of credit by or under the authority of, the United States, or any State, Territory, District, or municipal corporation, shall be appropriated to, or made or used for, the support of any school, educational or other institution, under the control of any religious or antireligious sect, organization, or denomination, or wherein the particular creed or tenets shall be read or taught in any school or institution supported in whole or in part by such revenue or loan of credit; and no such appropriation or loan of credit shall be made to any religious or anti-religious sect, organization, or denomination or to promote its interests or tenets. This article shall not be construed to prohibit the reading of the Bible in any school or institution; and it shall not have the effect to impair rights of property already vested. Congress shall have power by appropriate legislation to provide for the prevention and punishment of violations of this article."

This national defeat of the principle of no appropriation for private schools did not prevent the great majority of the states from writing it into their state constitutions and adopting laws against state aid for religious schools. At the present time most states also have laws against religious tests in education, against religious instruction, against the use of sectarian textbooks with numerous court decisions in favor of the secular educational ideal.

The pope continues to assert the Catholic ideal for American education:

"Now all this array of priceless educational treasures which we have barely touched upon, is so truly a property of the Church as to form her very substance, since she is the mystical body of Christ, the immaculate spouse of Christ, and consequently a most admirable mother and an incomparable and perfect teacher. This thought inspired St. Augustine, the great genius of whose blessed death we are about to celebrate the fifteenth centenary, with accents of tenderest love for so glorious a mother, 'O Catholic Church, true Mother of Christians! Not only dost thou preach to us, as is meet, how purely and chastely we are to worship God Himself, Whom to possess is life most blessed; thou dost moreover so cherish neighborly love and charity, that all the infirmities to which sinful souls are subject, find their most potent remedy in thee. Childlike thou art in moulding the child, strong with the young men, gentle with the aged, dealing with each according to his needs of mind and of body. Thou dost subject child to parent in a sort of free servitude, and settest parent over child in a jurisdiction of love. Thou bindest brethren to brethren by the bond of religion, stronger and closer than the bond of blood. * * * Thou unitest citizen to citizen, nation to nation, yea, all men, in a union not of companionship only, but of brotherhood, reminding them of their common origin. Thou teachest kings to care for their people, and biddest people to be subject to their kings. Thou teachest assiduously to whom honor is due, to whom love, to whom reverence, to whom fear, to whom comfort, to whom rebuke, to whom punishment; showing us that whilst not all things nor the same things are due to all, charity is due to all and offence to none.'"

It should also be remembered that Roman Catholicism teaches less than one-half its own population between 5-17 years of age in parish schools and that the Roman Catholic population of the United States for the last thirty years has been stabilized at approximately sixteen per cent. Beyond New England, in the various sections of the United States, the Roman Catholic per cent of population varies from around 3 to around 26.

What may be beginning of a new period in American state-church relations is the Hughes decision in the Louisiana text-book case. But it should be recalled that although the statute contemplated furnishing books to public school and private school pupils alike that, first, the *same books* were involved and, second, *none of the books was adapted to religious instruction.*

On July 14, 1936, the attorney-general of Iowa applied the principle of the Hughes decision to transportation of students in all schools:

". . . in applying the rule of law as announced by Chief Justice Hughes of the United States Supreme Court to the question (of free transportation of students in all schools) before us, we may likewise say that section 4179 of the code is a proper exercise of the taxing power of the State of Iowa, and it is used for a public purpose. Section 4179 of the code does not segregate children of school age within the district into classes of those attending private schools or the public school. Section 4179 of the code makes every child of school age living within said consolidated school corporation and more than a mile from such school the beneficiaries of this legislation. The private schools are not in any wise made the beneficiaries of this law. The intent of the legislature, as expressed in section 4179, was to make the school children and the State alone the beneficiaries of this law."

In spite of the Catholic contention that marriage is an affair of the Church, in the United States marriage and divorce, following Puritan practice, have always been under the jurisdiction of the state.

The best source-book on the general development of American life is H. S. Commager's *Documents of American History*: New York, 1938.

The selection of materials in this study is from:

1. Perly Poore, *The Federal and State Constitutions, Colonial Charters and Other Organic Laws of the United States.* Two volumes.   Washington, 1877.

2. Charles Kettleborough, *The State Constitutions . . .* Indianapolis, 1918.

3. The most recent constitutions of the forty-eight states.

4. Zaccaria Giacometti, *Quellen zur Geschichte der Trennung von Staat und Kirche*: Tuebingen, 1926.

5. P. G. Mode, *Source Book and Bibliographical Guide for American Church History*: Menasha, Wisconsin, 1921.

6. W. W. Hening, *Statutes at Large of Virginia.* 13 volumes, 1809-1823.

A

Religious References in the Charters and Constitutions of the Thirteen Colonies and Original States, A. D. 1584-1776.

I. VIRGINIA

1. Charter to Sir Walter Raleigh, 1584.

Poore, 1381.

> To determine to live together in Christian peace. . .

Laws are not to be against the true Christian faith now professed in the church of England. . .

2. First charter of Virginia, 1606.

Poore, 1888.

We, greatly commending and graciously accepting of their Desires for the furtherance of so noble a Work, which may, by the Providence of Almighty God, hereafter tend to the Glory of his Divine Majesty, in propagating of Christian Religion to such People, as yet live in Darkness and miserable Ignorance of the true Knowledge and Worship of God, and may in time bring the Infidels and Savages, living in those parts, to human Civility, and to a settled and quiet Government.

3. Articles, Instructions and Orders, Nov. 20, 1606.

Hening: Statutes at Large, I, 67-75.

> . . . And wee doe specially ordaine, charge, and require, the said presidents and councells, and the ministers of the said several colonies respectively, within their several limits and precincts, that they, with all diligence, care, and respect, doe provide, that the *true word, and service of God and Christian faith be preached, planted,* and *used,* not only within every of the said several colonies, and plantations, but alsoe as much as they may *amongst the salvage people,* which doe or shall adjoine unto them, or border upon them, according to the doctrine, rights, and religion now professed and established within our realme of England. . . . Furthermore, our will, and pleasure is, and wee doe hereby determine and ordaine, that every person and persons being our subjects of every the said colonies and plantations shall from time to time well entreate those salvages in

those parts, and use all good meanes to draw the *salvages and heathen people of the said several places,* and of the territories and countries adjoining to the true service and knowledge of God, and that all just, kind and charitable courses, shall be holden with such of them as shall conforme themselves to any good and sociable traffique and dealing with the subjects of us, our heires and successors, which shall be planted there, whereby they may be the sooner drawne to the true knowledge of God, and the obedience of us, our heares, and successors, under such severe paines and punishments, as shall be inflicted by the same several presidents and councells of the said several colonies, or the most part of them within their several limits and precincts, on such as shall offend therein, or doe the contrary. . . . .

4.   Second Charter of Virginia, 1609.

Poore, 1902.

And lastly, because the principal effect which we can desire or expect of this action is the conversion and reduction of the people in those parts unto the true worship of God and Christian religion, in which respect we should be loathe that any person should be permitted to pass that we suspected to affect the Superstitions of the Church of Rome, we do hereby declare, that it is our Will and Pleasure that none be permitted to pass in any Voyage from Time to Time to be made into said Country, but such as first shall have taken the Oath of Supremacy. . . .

5.   A True and Sincere Declaration of the Purpose and Ends of the Plantation begun in Virginia.

Brown, *Genesis of U. S.,* I. 339.

The principal and *Main Endes* (out of which are easily derived to any meane understanding infinitnesse, and yet great ones) *were first to preach and baptize into Christian Religion, and by propagation of the Gospell, to recover out of the armes of the Divell, a number of poore and miserable soules,* wrapt up unto death, in almost invincible ignorance; to endeavour the fulfilling, and accomplishment of the number of the elect, which shall be gathered from out all corners of the earth; and to add our myte to the Treasury of Heaven, that as we pray for the coming of the Kingdome of Glory, so to expresse in our actions, the same desire, if God, have pleased, to use so weak instruments, to the ripening and consummation thereof.

6.   Third Charter of Virginia, 1611-12.

Poore, 1902.

James . . . as well Adventurers as Planters of the first colony in Virginia, and for the propagation of Christian Religion, and Reclaiming of People barbarous, to Civility and Humanity, We have . . .

II. MASSACHUSETTS

7.   The Charter of New England, 1620.

Poore, 921.

James . . . We according to our princely Inclination, favoring much their worthy Disposition, in Hope thereby to advance the in Largement of Christian Religion, to the Glory of God Almighty, as also by that Meanes to stretch out the Bounds of our Dominions, and to replenish those Deserts with People governed by Lawes and Magistrates, for the peaceable Commerce of all . . .

In Contemplacion and serious Consideration whereof, Wee have thought it fitt according to our Kingly Duty, soe much as in Us lyeth, to second and followe God's sacred Will, rendering reverend Thanks to his Divine Majestie for his gracious favour in laying open and revealing the same unto us, before any other Christian Prince or State, by which Meanes without Offence, and We trust to his Glory, Wee may with Boldness goe on to the settling of soe hopeful a Work which tendeth to the reducing and Conversion of such Savages as remain wandering in Desolacion and Distress, to Civil Societie and Christian Religion, to the Inlargement of our own Dominions . . .

8.   Agreement between the Settlers at New Plymouth, Nov. 11, 1620.

Poore, 931.

In the Name of God, Amen. . . . Having undertaken for the Glory of God and Advancement of the Christian Faith, and the Honour of our King and Country, a Voyage to plant the first Colony in the Northern Parts of Virginia . . .

9.   Charter of Massachusetts Bay, 1629.

Poore, 940.

. . . and for the directing, ruling, and disposeing of all other

Matters and Thinges, whereby our said People, Inhabitants there, may be soe religiously, peaceablie, and civilly governed, as their good Life and orderlie Convercason, maie wynn and incite the Natives of the Country, to the Knowledge and Obedience of the onlie true God and Savior of Mankinde, and the Christian Fayth, which in our Royall Intencon and the Adventurers free Profession, is the principal Ende of this Plantacion.

10. The Charter of Massachusetts Bay, 1691.
Poore, 950.

... Wee doe by these presents for us Our heires and Successors Grant Establish and Ordaine that for ever hereafter there shall be a liberty of Conscience allowed in the Worship of God to all Christians (Except Papists) Inhabiting or which shall Inhabit or be Resident within our said Province or Territory . . .
. . . and to dispose of matters and things whereby our Subjects inhabitants of our said Province may be Religiously peaceably and Civilly Governed, Protected and Defended soe as their good life and orderly Conversation may win the Indians Natives of the Country to the knowledge and obedience of the onely true God and Saviour of Mankinde and the Christian Faith which his Royall Majestie our Royall Grandfather king Charles the first in his said Letters Patents declared was his Royall Intentions and the Adventurers free Possession to be the Princepall end of the said Plantation and for the better secureing and maintaining Liberty of Conscience hereby granted to all persons at any time being and resideing within our said Province or Territory as aforesaid . . .

11. Explanatory Charter of Massachusetts Bay, 1726.
Poore, 954.   Contains no reference to religion.

III MARYLAND

12. Charter of Maryland, 1632.
Poore, 810.

Charles, by the grace of God, of *England, Scotland, France, and Ireland,* King, Defender of the Faith, &c. To all to whom these Presents shall come, Greeting:

II. Whereas our well beloved and right trusty Subject Caecillius Calvert, Baron of Baltimore, in our Kingdom of

Ireland, son and Heir of George Calvert, Knight, late Baron of Baltimore, in our said Kingdom of *Ireland,* treading in the Steps of his Father, being animated with a laudable, and pious Zeal for extending the *Christian Religion* and also the Territories of our Empire, hath humbly besought leave of Us, that he may transport, by his own Industry, and Expence, a numerous Colony of the *English* Nation, to a certain Region, herein after described, in a Country hitherto uncultivated, in the Parts of *America,* and partly occupied by Savages, having no Knowledge of the Divine Being, and that all that Region, with some certain Privileges, and Jurisdictions, appertaining unto the wholesome Government, and State of his Colony and Region aforesaid, may by our Royal Highness be given, granted, and confirmed unto him, and his Heirs. . . .

IV.   Also We do Grant, and likewise confirm unto the said Baron of Baltimore, . . . all Islands and Islets within the Limits aforesaid, all and singular the Islands and Islets, from the Eastern Shore of the aforesaid Region, towards the East, which have been, or shall be formed in the Sea, situate within Ten marine Leagues from the said Shore; . . . And furthermore the Patronages and Advowsons of all Churches which (with the increasing Worship and Religion of Christ) within the said Region . . ., hereafter shall happen to be built, together with Licene and Faculty of erecting and founding Churches, Chapels, and Places of Worship, in convenient and suitable places, within the Premises, and of causing the same to be dedicated and consecrated according to the Ecclesiastical Laws of our Kingdom of *England,* with all, and singular such, and as ample Rights, Jurisdictions, Privileges, Prerogatives, Royalties, Liberties, Immunities, and royal Rights, and temporal Franchises whatsoever, as well by Sea as by Land, within the Region . . . aforesaid, to be had, exercised, used, and enjoyed, as any Bishop of Durham, within the Bishoprick or County Palatine of Durham, in our Kingdom of *England,* ever heretofore hath had, held, used, or enjoyed, or of Right could, or ought to have, hold, use, or enjoy.

IV. CONNECTICUT

13.   Fundamental Orders of Connecticut, 1638-1639.
Poore, 249, 252.
Forasmuch as it hath pleased the Almighty God by the wise

disposition of his diuyne pruidence so to Order and dispose of things that we the Inhabitants and Residents of Windsor, Harteford and Wethersfield are now cohabiting and dwelling in and vppon the River of Conectecotte and the Lands thereunto adioyneing; And well knowing where a people are gathered together the word of God requires that to mayntayne the peace and vnion of such a people there should be an orderly and decent Gouerment established according to God, to order and dispose of the affayres of the people at all seasons as occation shall require; doe therefore assotiate and conioyne our selues to be as one Publike State or Commonwelth; and doe, for our selues and our Successors and such as shall be adioyned to vs att any tyme hereafter, enter into Combinatioin and Confederation togather, to mayntayne and prsearue the liberty and purity of the gospell of our Lord Jesus which we now professe, as also the disciplyne of the Churches, which according to the truth of the said gospell is now practised amongst vs; As also in our Ciuell Affaires to be guided and gouerned according to such Lawes, Rules, Orders and decrees as shall be made, ordered & decreed, as followeth . . .

THE OATH OF A MAGISTRATE, FOR THE PRESENT

I, N . . . W . . ., being chosen a Magestrate within this Jurisdiction for the yeare ensueing, doe sweare by the great and dreadful name of the euerliueing God, to promote the publike good and peace of the same, according to the best of my skill, and that I will mayntayne all the lawfull priuiledges thereof according to my vnderstanding, as also assist in the execution of all such wholsome lawes as are made or shall be made by lawfull authority heare established, and will further the execution of Justice for the tyme aforesaid according to the righteous rule of Gods word; so help me God, etc.

14.   Connecticut Code of 1672.

Mode, 104.

. . . It is therefore Ordered by the Authority of this Court, That if any Christian so called, within this Colony, shall contemptuously behave himself towards the Word preached, or the messengers thereof, called to Dispense the same in any Congregation, when he doth Faithfully execute his service and Office therein, according to the Will and Word of God; either by

Interrupting him in his Preaching, or by charging him falsly with an Errour, which he hath not taught, in the open face of the Church; or like a Son of Korah cast upon his true Doctrine or himself, any reproach to the dishonour of the Lord Jesus Who hath sent him, and to the disparagement of that his holy Ordinance and makeing Gods wayes contemptible and rediculous: That every such person or persons (whatsoever Censure the Church may pass) shall for the first scandall be convented and reproved openly by the Magistrate in some publick Assembly, and bound to their good behaviour. And if a Second time they break forth into the like contemptuous carriages, they shall either pay *five pounds* to the publick, or stand two hours openly vpon a block or stool four foot high upon a publick meeting day, with a paper fixed on his Breast written with Capital Letters, AN OPEN AND OBSTINATE CONTEMNER OF GODS HOLY ORDINANCES, that others may fear and be ashamed of breaking out into the like wickedness.

It is further Orderd; That wheresoever the Ministry of the Word is established according to the order of the Gospel throughout this Colony, every person shall duely resort and attend thereunto respectively upon the Lords day, and upon such publick Fast dayes, and dayes of thanksgiving, as are to be generally kept by the appointment of Authority. And if any person within this Jurisdiction, shall without just and necessary cause, withdraw himself from hearing the publick Ministry of the Word, after due means of conviction used, he shall forfeit for his absence from every such meeting *five shillings;* all such offences to be heard and determined by any one Magistrate or more from time to time; provided all breaches of this Law be complained of, and prosecuted to effect within one moneth after the same. . . .

V.   RHODE ISLAND

15.   Patent for Providence Plantations, 1643.
Poore, 1595.
. . . a free Charter of Civil Incorporation and Government . . . Together with full Power and Authority to rule themselves, and such others as shall hereafter inhabit within any Part of the said Tract of land, by such a Form of Civil Government, as by voluntary consent of all, or the greater Part of them, they shall find most suitable to their Estate and Condition . . .

16.   Charter of Rhode Island and Providence Plantations, 1663.
Poore, 1596ff.

. . . that they, persuing, with peaceable and loyall mindes,
their sober, serious and religious intentions, of godlie edifieing
themselves, and one another, in the holie Christian ffaith and
worshipp as they were perswaded; together with the gaineing
over and conversione of the poore ignorant, Indian natives, in
those partes of America, to the sincere professione and obedi-
enc of same ffaith and worshipp. . . .

. . . Now know yee, that wee beinge willinge to encourage
the hopeful undertaking of oure sayd loyall and loveing subjects, and to secure them in the free exercise and enjoyment of
all theire civill and religious rights, appertaining to them, as
our loveing subjects; and to preserve unto them that libertye,
in the true Christian ffaith and worshipp of God, which they
have sought with soe much travaill, and with peaceable myndes,
and loyall subjectione to our royall progenitors and ourselves,
to enjoye; and because some of the people and inhabitants of
the same colonie cannot, in theire private opinions, conforme
to the publique exercise of religion, according to the litturgy,
formes and ceremonyes of the Church of England, or take or
subscribe the oaths and articles made and established in that
behalfe; and for that the same, by reason of the remote dis-
tances of those places; will (as wee hope) bee noe breach of the
unitie and unifformitie established in this nation: Have therefore thought ffit, and doe hereby publish, graunt, ordeyne and
declare, That our royall will and pleasure is, that noe person
within the sayd coloyne, at any tyme hereafter, shall be any
wise molested, punished, disquieted, or called in question, for any
differences in opinione in matters of religion, and doe not actually disturb the civill peace of our sayd colony; but that all
and everye person and persons may, from tyme to tyme, and
at all tymes hereafter, freelye and fullye have and enjoy his
and theire owne judgments and consciences, in matters of religious concernments, throughout the tract of lande hereafter
mentioned; they behaving themselves peaceablie and quietlie,
and not useing this libertie to lycentiousnesse and profanesse,
nor to the civill injurye or outward disturbeance of others; any
lawe, statute, or clause, therein contayned, or to bee contayned,
usage or custome of this realme, to the contrary hereof, in any
wise, not withstanding.   And that they may bee in the better

capacity to defend themselves, in theire just rights and liber-
tyes against in the enemies of the Christian ffaith, and others, in
all respects, wee have further thought flt, and at the humble petition of the persons aforesayd are gratiously pleasead to declare, That they shall have and enjoye the benefitt of our late
act of indempnity and ffree pardon, as the rest of our subjects
in other our dominions and territoryes have; and to create and
make them a bodye politique or corporate, with the powers and
privileges hereinafter mentioned. . . .[1]

VI. NORTH CAROLINA

17. Charter of Carolina, 1663.

Poore, 1383.

And furthermore, the patronage and advowsons of all the
churches and chapels, which as Christian religion shall increase
within the country, isles, islets and limits aforesaid, shall happen
hereafter to be erected, together with license and power to build
and found churches, chappels and oratories, in convenient and
fit places, within the said bounds and limits, and to cause them

---

1 Orrin Bishop Judd in The Colgate-Rochester Bulletin, December, 1937, p. 87:
  In the Meeting at Newport, March 1, 1663, when the Charter of Charles II.,
was accepted, the General Assembly passed an act in these words:
  ''That all men professing Christianity, and of competent estates, and of
civil conversation, who acknowledge and are obedient to the civil magistrates,
though of differnt judgments in religious affairs (Roman Catholics only excepted), shall be admitted freemen, and shall have liberty to choose and be
chosen officers in the Colony, both military and civil.''
  This appears of record in the first collection of the statutes of Rhode Island,
which was prepared by a committee in 1703, and in the digests of 1719, 1731,
and 1767, (see Vol. 2, Rhode Island Colonial Records p. 36 and note), and is
put beyond all question by an act of the General Assembly, repealing in 1783
the anti-catholic law of 1663, to wit:
  ''That all the rights and privileges of the Protestant citizens of this state,
as declared in and by an Act made and passed the 1st day of March, A. D.
1663, be, and the same are hereby fully extended to Roman Catholic citizens;
and that they, being of competent estates and of civil conversation, and acknowledging and paying obedience to the civil magistrates shall be admitted freemen,
and shall have liberty to choose and be chosen civil or military officers within
this State, any exception in the said Act to the contrary notwithstanding.'' See
Col. Records, vol. 9, p. 674.
  It is stated by Francis Brinley, as recorded in Holmes's American Annals,
vol. I, p. 341, that
  ''in 1665 the government and council of Rhode Island, &c., passed an order
for outlawing the people called Quakers, because they would not bear arms, and
to seize their estates; but the people in general rose up against these severe
orders, and would not suffer it.''
  Hon. Samuel Eddy, for many years Secretary of State in Rhode Island,
while he claims that Brinley's statement in reference to the Quakers is ''incor-
rect and partial,'' admits it to be, after all, substantially true.

to be dedicated and consecrated according to the ecclesiastical laws of our kingdom of England, together with all and singular the like, and as ample rights, jurisdictions, privileges, prerogatives, royalties, liberties, immunities, and franchises of what kind soever, within the countries, isles, islets and limits aforesaid.

18. Charter of Carolina, 1665.

Poore, 1397.

... And that no person or persons unto whom such liberty shall be given, shall be any way molested, punished, disquieted, or called in question, for any differences in opinion, or practice in matters of religious concernments, who do not actually disturb the civil peace of the province, county or colony, that they shall make their abode in: But all and every such person and persons may from time to time, and at all times, freely and quietly have and enjoy his and their judgments and consciences, in matters of religion, throughout all the said province or colony, they behaving themselves peaceably, and not using this liberty to licentiousness, nor to the civil injury, or outward disturbance of others: Any law, statute, or clause, contained or to be contained, usage or custom of our realm of England, to the contrary hereof, in any-wise, notwithstanding.

19. Fundamental Constitutions of Carolina, 1669.

Poore, 1406.

Ninety-five. No man shall be permitted to be a freeman of Carolina or to have any estate or habitation within it, that doth not acknowledge a God; and that God is publicly and solemnly to be worshipped.

Ninety-six. [As the country comes to be sufficiently planted and distributed into fit divisions, it shall belong to the parliament to take care for the building of churches, and the public maintenance of divines, to be employed in the exercise of religion, according to the Church of England; which being the only true and orthodox, and the national religion of all the King's dominions, is so also of Carolina; and, therefore, it alone shall be allowed to receive public maintenance, by grant of parliament.]

Ninety-seven. But since the natives of that place, who will be concerned in our plantation, are utterly strangers to Christianity, whose idolatry, ignorance, or mistake gives us no right to expel or use them ill; and those who remove from other parts to plant there will unavoidably be of different opinions concerning matters of religion, the liberty whereof they will expect to have allowed them, and it will not be reasonable for us, on this account, to keep them out, that civil peace may be maintained amidst diversity of opinions, and our agreement and compact with all men may be duly and faithfully observed; the violation whereof, upon what pretence soever, cannot be without great offence to Almighty God, and great scandal to the true religion which we profess; and also that Jews, heathens, and other dissenters from the purity of Christian religion may not be scared and kept at a distance from it, but, by having an opportunity of acquainting themselves with the truth and reasonableness of its doctrines, and the peaceableness and inoffensiveness of its professors, may, by good usage and persuasion, and all those convincing methods of gentleness and meekness, suitable to the rules and design of the gospel, be won ever to embrace and unfeignedly receive the truth; therefore, any seven or more persons agreeing in any religion, shall constitute a church or profession, to which they shall give some name, to distinguish it from others.

Ninety-eight.   The terms of admittance and communion with any church or profession shall be written in a book, and therein be subscribed by all the members of the said church or profession; which book shall be kept by the public register of the precinct wherein they reside.

Ninety-nine.   The time of every one's subscription and admittance shall be dated in the said book or religious record.

One hundred.   In the terms of communion of every church or profession, these following shall be three; without which no agreement or assembly of men, upon pretence of religion, shall be accounted a church or profession within these rules:

1st.   "That there is a God."

II.   "That God is publicly to be worshipped."

III. "That it is lawful and the duty of every man, being thereunto called by those that govern, to bear witness to truth; and that every church or profession shall, in their terms of communion, set down the external way whereby they witness a truth as in the presence of God, whether it be by laying hands on or kissing the bible, as in the Church of England, or by holding up the hand, or any other sensible way."

One hundred and one.   No person above seventeen years of age shall have any benefit or protection of the law, or be capable of any place of profit or honor, who is not a member of some church or profession, having his name recorded in some one, and but one religious record at once.

One hundred and two.   No person of any other church or profession shall disturb or molest any religious assembly.

One hundred and three.   No person whatsoever shall speak anything in their religious assembly irreverently or seditiously of the government or governors, or of state matters.

One hundred and four.   Any person subscribing the terms of communion, in the record of the said church or profession, before the precinct register, and any five members of the said church or profession, shall be thereby made a member of the said church or profession.

One hundred and five.   Any person striking out his own name out of any religious record, or his name being struck out by any officer thereunto authorized by each church or profession respectively, shall cease to be a member of that church or profession.

One hundred and six.   No man shall use any reproachful, reviling, or abusive language against any religion of any church or profession; that being the certain way of disturbing the peace, and of hindering the conversion of any to the truth, by engaging them in quarrels and animosities, to the hatred of the professors and that profession which otherwise they might be brought to assent to.

One hundred and seven.   Since charity obliges us to wish well to the souls of all men, and religion ought to alter nothing in any man's civil estate or right, it shall be lawful for slaves, as well as others, to enter themselves, and be of what church or profession any of them shall think best, and, therefore, be as fully members as any freeman.   But yet no slave shall hereby be exempted from that civil dominion his master hath over him, but be in all things in the same state and condition he was in before.

One hundred and eight.   Assemblies, upon what pretence soever of religion, not observing and performing the above said rules, shall not be esteemed as churches, but unlawful meetings, and be punished as other riots.

One hundred and nine.   No person whatsoever shall disturb, molest, or persecute another for his speculative opinions in religion, or his way of worship.

One hundred and ten. Every freeman of Carolina shall have absolute power and authority over his negro slaves, of what opinion or religion soever.

VII.   SOUTH CAROLINA

See number 17 and 18.

VIII.   NEW JERSEY

20.   Royal Grant to the Duke of York, 1664 and 1674.

21.   Grant of New Jersey 1664 and Concessions of 1664-65. Poore, 1310 and 783f., 786f.

Religious references lacking. The reconveyance of the Duke of York, August 6, 1680, provided for liberty of conscience in West New Jersey:

There is likewise Certain Provision made for the Liberty of Conscience in Matters of Religion, that all Persons living Peaceably may injoy the Benefit of the Religious Exercise thereof without any Molestation whatsoever.[1]

IX.   NEW YORK

See 20.

X.   NEW HAMPSHIRE

22.   Commission for New Hampshire, 1680. Poore, 1277.

. . . And above all things We do by these presents will, require and command our said Councill to take all possible care for ye discountenancing of vice and encouraging of virtue and good living; and that by such examples ye infidle may be invited and desire to partake of ye Christian Religion, and for ye greater ease and satisfaction of ye said loving subjects in matters of religion, We do hereby require and command ye liberty of conscience shall be allowed unto all protestants; yet such es-

---

1 A. C. Myers, Ed.—Narratives of Early Pennsylvania, West New Jersey and Delaware, A. D. 1630-1707, p. 193.

pecially as shall be conformable to ye rites of ye Church of England shall be particularly countenanced and encouraged. . . .

XI. PENNSYLVANIA

23. Charter for the Province of Pennsylvania, 1681.

Poore, 1515.

And Our further pleasure is, and wee doe hereby, for us, our heires and Successors, charge and require, that if any of the inhabitants of the said Province, to the number of Twenty, shall at any time hereafter be desirous, and shall by any writeing, or by any person deputed for them, signify such their desire to the Bishop of *London* that any preacher or preachers, to be approved of by the said Bishop, may be sent unto them for their instruction, that then such preacher or preachers shall and may be and reside within the said Province, without any deniall or molestation whatsoever.

24. Frame of Government of Pennsylvania, 1682.

Poore, 1526.

XXXV. That all persons living in this province, who confess and acknowledge the one Almighty and eternal God, to be the Creator, Upholder and Ruler of the world; and that hold themselves obliged in conscience to live peaceably and justly in civil society, shall, in no ways, be molested or prejudiced for their religious persuasion, or practice, in matters of faith and worship, nor shall they be compelled, at any time, to frequent or maintain any religious worship, place or ministry whatever.

XXXVI. That, according to the good example of the primitive Christians, and the case of the creation, every first day of the week, called the Lord's day, people shall abstain from their common daily labour, that they may the better dispose themselves to worship God according to their understandings.

XXXVII. That as a careless and corrupt administration of justice draws the wrath of God upon magistrates, so the wildness and looseness of the people provoke the indignation of God against a country: therefore, that all such offences against God, as swearing, cursing, lying, prophane talking, drunkenness, drinking of healths, obscene words, incest, sodomy, rapes, whoredom, fornication, and other uncleanness (not to be repeated) all treasons, misprisons, murders, duel, felony, seditions, maims, forcible entries, and other violences, to the persons and estates of the inhabitants within this province; all prizes, stage-players, cards, dice, May-games, gamesters, masques, revels, bull-baitings, cock-fightings, bear-baitings, and the like, which excite the people to rudeness, cruelty, looseness, and irreligion, shall be respectively discouraged, and severely punished, according to the appointment of the Governor and freemen in provincial Council and General Assembly; as also all proceedings contrary to these laws, that are not here made expressly penal.

25.   Frame of Government of Pennsylvania, 1696. Poore, 1533.

And whereas divers persons within this government, cannot, for conscience sake, take an oath, upon any account whatsoever, Be it therefore enacted by the authority aforesaid, That all and every such person and persons being at any time hereafter, required, upon lawful occasion, to give evidence, or take an oath, in any case whatsoever, shall, instead of swearing, be permitted to make his, or their solemn affirmation, attest, or declaration, which shall be adjudged, and is hereby enacted and declared to be of the same force and effect, to all intents and purposes whatsoever, as if they had taken an oath; and in case any such person or persons shall be lawfully convicted of having wilfully and corruptly affirmed, or declared any matter or thing, upon such solemn affirmation or attest, shall incur the same penalties and forfeitures as by the laws and statutes of *England* are provided against persons convicted of wilfull and corrupt perjury.

And be it further enacted by the authority aforesaid, That all persons who shall be hereafter either elected to serve in Council and Assembly, or commissionated or appointed to be Judges, Justices, Masters of the Rolls, Sheriffs, Coroners, and all other offices of State and trust, within this government, who shall conscientiously scruple to take an oath, but when lawfully required, will make and subscribe the declaration and profession of their Christian belief, according to the late act of parliament made in the first year of king *William,* and the late queen *Mary,* entitled, An act for exempting their majesties' Protestant subjects, dissenting from the Church of *England,* from the penalty of certain laws, shall be adjudged, and are hereby declared to be qualified to act in their said respective offices and places, and thereupon the several officers herein mentioned, shall, instead of an oath make their solemn affirmation of declaration in manner and form following; . . .

26.   Charter of Privileges, 1701.

Poore, 1537.

BECAUSE no People can be truly happy, though under the greatest Enjoyment of Civil Liberties, if abridged of the Freedom of their Consciences, as to their Religious Profession and Worship: And Almighty God being the only Lord of Conscience, Father of Lights and Spirits; and the Author as well as Object of all divine Knowledge, Faith and Worship, who only doth enlighten the Minds, and persuade and convince the Understandings of People, I do hereby grant and declare, That no Person or Persons, inhabiting in this Province or Territories, who shall confess and acknowledge *One* almighty God, the Creator, Upholder and Ruler of the World; and profess him or themselves obliged to live quietly under the Civil Government, shall be in any Case molested or prejudiced, in his or their Person or Estate, because of his or their conscientious Persuasion or Practice, nor be compelled to frequent or maintain any religious Worship, Place or Ministry, contrary to his or their Mind, or to do or suffer any other Act or Thing, contrary to their religious Persuasion.

AND that all Persons who also profess to believe in *Jesus Christ,* the Savior of the World, shall be capable (notwithstanding their other Persuasions and Practices in Point of Conscience and Religion) to serve this Government in any Capacity both legislatively and executively, he or they solemnly promising, when lawfully required, Allegiance to the King as Sovereign, and Fidelity to the Proprietary and Governor, and taking the Attests as now established by the Law made at *New-Castle,* in the Year *One Thousand and Seven Hundred,* entitled, *An Act directing the Attests of several Officers and Ministers,* as now amended and confirmed this present Assembly.

BUT because the happiness of Mankind depends so much upon the Enjoying of Liberty of their Consciences as aforesaid, I do hereby solemnly declare, promise and grant, for me, my Heirs and Assigns, That the *First* Article of this Charter relating to Liberty of Conscience, and every Part and Clause therein, according to the true Intent and Meaning thereof, shall be kept and remain, without any Alteration, inviolably for ever.

XII. DELAWARE

27. Charter of Delaware, 1701.

Poore, 270.

BECAUSE no People can be truly happy, though under the greatest Enjoyment of Civil Liberties, if abridged of the Freedom of their Consciences, as to their Religious Profession and Worship: And Almighty God being the only Lord of Conscience, Father of Lights and Spirits; and the Author as well as object of all divine Knowledge, Faith and Worship, who only doth enlighten the Minds, and persuade and convince the Understandings of People, I do hereby grant and declare, That no Person or Persons, inhabiting in this province or Territories, who shall confess and acknowledge *One* Almighty God, the Creator, Upholder and Ruler of the World; and professes him or themselves obliged to live quietly under the Civil Government, shall be in any Case molested or prejudiced, in his or their Person or Estate, because of his or their conscious Persuasion or Practice, nor be compelled to frequent or maintain any religious Worship, Place or Ministry, contrary to his or their Mind, or to do or suffer any other Act or Thing, contrary to their religious Persuasion.

AND that all Persons who also profess to believe in *Jesus Christ,* the Saviour of the World, shall be capable (notwithstanding their own Persuasion and Practices in Point of Conscience and Religion) to serve this Government in any Capacity, both legislatively and executively, he or they solemnly promising, when lawfully required, Allegiance to the King as Sovereign, and Fidelity to the Proprietary and Governor, and taking the Attests as now established by the Law made at *Newcastle,* in the Year *One Thousand Seven Hundred,* entituled, *An Act directing the Attests of several Officers and Ministers,* as now amended and confirmed this present Assembly.

BUT, because the Happiness of Mankind depends so much upon the Enjoying of Liberty of their Consciences, as aforesaid, I do hereby solemnly declare, promise and grant, for me, my Heirs and Assigns, That the *First* Article of this Charter relating to Liberty of Conscience, and every Part and Clause therein, according to the true Intent and Meaning thereof, shall be kept and remain, without any Alteration, inviolably for ever.

XIII. GEORGIA

28. Charter of Georgia, 1732.

Poore, 375.

. . . And for the greater ease and encouragement of our loving subjects and such others as shall come to inhabit in our said colony, we do by these presents, for us, our heirs and successors, grant, establish and ordain, that forever hereafter, there shall be a liberty of conscience allowed in the worship of God, to all persons inhabiting, or which shall inhabit or be resident within our said province, and that all such persons, except papists, shall have a free exercise of religion, so they be contented with the quiet and peaceable enjoyment of the same, not giving offence or scandal to the government. . . .

ART. VI. The representatives shall be chosen out of the residents in each county, who shall have resided at least twelve months in this State, and three months in the county where they shall be elected; except the freeholders of the counties of Glynn and Camden, who are in a state of alarm, and who shall have the liberty of choosing one member each, as specified in the articles of this constitution, in any other county, until they have residents sufficient to qualify them fore more; and they shall be of the Protestant religion, and of the age of twenty-one years, and shall be possessed in their own right of two hundred and fifty acres of land, or some property to the amount of two hundred and fifty pounds.

B.

RELIGIOUS REFERENCES IN STATE DOCUMENTS OF THE REVOLUTIONARY PERIOD, A. D. 1776-1791

I. VIRGINIA

29. Virginia Declaration of Rights, June 12, 1776.

Poore, 1909.

Section 16. That religion, or the duty which we owe to our Creator, and the manner of discharging it, can be directed only by reason and by conviction, not by force or violence; and therefore, all men are equally entitled to the free exercise of residents sufficient to qualify them for more; and they shall be the mutual duty of all to practice Christian forbearance, love, and charity towards each other.

30. Constitution of Virginia, June 29, 1776.

Poore, 1910.

No mention of God or religion.

31. Virginia Bill for Establishing Religious Freedom, 1786.

Hening XII, 84ff.

I. WHEREAS Almighty God hath created the mind free; that all attempts to influence it by temporal punishments or burthens, or by civil incapacitations, tend only to beget habits of hypocrisy and meanness, and are a departure from the plan of the Holy author of our religion, who being Lord both of body and mind, yet chose not to propagate it by coercions on either, as was in his Almighty power to do; that the impious presumption of legislators and rulers civil as well as ecclesiastical, who being themselves but fallible and uninspired men, have assumed dominion over the faith of others, setting up their own opinions and modes of thinking as the only true and infallible, and as such endeavoring to impose them on others, hath established and maintained false religions over the greatest part of the world, and through all time; that to compel a man to furnish contributions of money for the propagation of opinions which he disbelieves, is sinful and tyrannical; that even the forcing him to support this or that teacher of his own religious persuasion, is depriving him of the comfortable liberty of giving his contributions to the particular pastor whose morals he would make his pattern, and whose powers he feels most persuasive to righteousness, and is withdrawing from the ministry those temporary rewards, which proceeding from an approbation of their personal conduct are an additional incitement to earnest and unremitting labours for the instruction of mankind; that our civil rights have no dependence on our religious opinions, any more than our opinions in physics or geometry; that therefore the proscribing any citizen as unworthy the public confidence by laying upon him an incapacity of being called to offices of trust and emolument, unless he profess or renounce this or that religious opinion, is depriving him injuriously of those privileges and advantages to which in common with his fellow-citizens he has a natural right; that it tends only to corrupt the principles of that religion it is meant to encourage, by bribing with a monopoly of worldly honours and emoluments, those who will externally profess and conform to it; that though indeed these are criminal who do not withstand such temptation, yet neither are those innocent who lay the bait in their way; that to suffer the civil magistrate to intrude his powers into the field of opinion, and to restrain the profession or propagation of principles on supposition of their ill tendency, is a dangerous fallacy, which at once destroys all religious liberty, because he being of course judge of that tendency will make his opinions the rule of judgment, and approve or condemn the sentiments of others only as they shall square with or differ from his own; that it is time enough for the rightful purpose of civil government, for its officers to interfere when principles break out into overt acts against peace and good order; and finally that truth is great and will prevail if left to herself, that she is the proper and sufficient antagonist to error, and has nothing to fear from the conflict, unless by human interposition disarmed of her natural weapons, free argument and debate, errors ceasing to be dangerous when it is permitted freely to contradict them.

II. *Be it enacted by the General Assembly,* that no man shall be compelled to frequent or support any religious worship, place or ministry whatsoever, nor shall be enforced, restrained, molested, or burthened in his body or goods, nor shall otherwise suffer on account of his religious opinions or belief; but that all men shall be free to profess, and by argument to maintain, their opinion in matters of religion, and that the same shall in no wise diminish, enlarge or affect their civil capacities.

III.   And though we well know that this assembly, elected by the people for the ordinary purposes of legislation only, have no power to restrain the acts of succeeding assemblies, constituted with powers equal to our own, and that therefore to declare this act to be irrevocable would be of no effect in law; yet as we are free to declare, and do declare, that the rights hereby asserted are of the natural rights of mankind, and that if any act shall hereafter be passed to repeal the present, or to narrow its operation, such act will be an infringement of natural right.

II.   MASSACHUSETTS

32.   Constitution of Massachusetts, 1780.

Poore, 956.

From the Preamble

. . . acknowledging with grateful hearts, the goodness of the Great Legislator, of the universe . . and devoutly imploring His direction. . .

Art. 2.   It is the right as well as the Duty of all men in society, publickly and at stated seasons to worship the Supreme Being, the great Creator and preserver of the Universe.   And no subject shall be hurt, molested, or restrained, in his person, liberty, or estate, for worshipping God in the manner and season most agreeable to the dictates of his own conscience, or public peace, or obstruct others in their religious worship.

Art. 3.   As the happiness of a people, and the good order and preservation of civil government, essentially depend upon piety, religion, and morality: and as these cannot be generally diffused through a Community, but by the institution of the public worship of God, and of public instructions in piety, religion, and morality: Therefore to promote their happiness and to secure the good order and preservation of their government, the people of this Commonwealth have a right to invest the Legislature with power to authorize and require, and the Legislature shall, from time to time, authorize and require the several towns, parishes, precincts and other bodies politic, or religious societies, to make suitable provision, at their own expense, for the institution of the public worship of God, and for the support and maintenance of public protestant teachers of piety, religion and morality, in all cases where such provision shall be made voluntarily.—And the people of this Commonwealth have also a right to, and do, invest their Legislature with authority to enjoin upon all subjects an attendance upon the instructions of the public teachers aforesaid, at stated times and seasons, if there be any on whose instructions they can conscientiously and conveniently attend—Provided notwithstanding that the several towns, parishes, precincts, and other bodies politic, or religious societies, shall, at all times, have the exclusive right of electing their public teachers, and of contracting with them for their support and maintenance.—And all monies paid by the Subject to the support of public worship, and of the public teachers aforesaid, shall, if he require it, be uniformly applied to the support of the public teacher or teachers of the parish or pre--cinct in which the said monies are raised.—And every denomina-tion of Christians, demeaning themselves peaceably, and as Good subjects of the Commonwealth, shall be equally under the protection of the Law; and no subordination of any one sect or denomination to another shall ever be established by Law.

Chapter II Section I Art. III. Governor . . .
. . . and unless he shall declare himself to be of the Christian religion [See Chapter II Section II Art. I for Lieutenant-Governor].

Chapter VI. Art. I.

I, A. B., do declare that I believe the Christian Religion, and have a firm persuasion of its truth; . . .
Provided always, that when any person or appointed as afore-said shall be of the denomination of the people called Quakers, and shall decline taking the said oath(s) he shall make his affirm-ation in the foregoing form.

III. MARYLAND

33. Constitution of Maryland, 1776.
Poore, 819.

XXXIII. That, as it is the duty of every man to worship God in such manner as he thinks most acceptable to him; all persons, professing the Christian religion, are equally entitled to protection in their religious liberty; wherefore no person ought by any law to be molested in his person or estate on account of his religious persuasion or profession, or for his religious practice; unless, under colour of religion, any man shall disturb the good order, peace or safety of the State, or shall infringe the laws of morality, or injure others, in their natural, civil, or religious rights; nor ought any person to be compelled to frequent or maintain, or contribute, unless on contract, to maintain any particular place of worship, or any particular ministry; yet the Legislature may, in their discretion, lay a general and equal tax, for the support of the Christian religion; leaving to each individual the power of appointing the payment over of the money, collected from him, to the support of any particular place of worship or minister, or for the benefit of the poor of his own denomination, or the worship of minister, or for the benefit of the poor of his own denomination, or the poor in general of any particular county: But the churches, chapels, glebes, and all other property now belonging to the church of England, ought to remain to the church of England forever. And all acts of Assembly, lately passed, for collecting monies for building or repairing particular churches or chapels of ease, shall continue in force, and be executed, unless the Legislature shall, by act, supersede or repeal the same: but no county court shall assess any quantity of tobacco, or sum of money, hereafter, on the application of any vestry-men or church-wardens; and every encumbent of the church of England, who hath remained in his parish, and performed his duty, shall be entitled to receive the provision and support established by the act, entitled "An act for the support of the clergy of the church of England, in this Province," till the November court of this present year, to be held for the county in which his parish shall lie, or partly lie, or for such time as hath remained in this parish, and performed his duty.

XXXIV. That every gift, sale, or devise of lands, to any minister, public teacher, or preacher of the gospel, as such, or to any religious sect, order or denomination, or to or for the support, use or benefit of, or in trust for, any minister, public teacher, or preacher of the gospel, as such, or any religious sect order or denomination—and every gift or sale of goods, or chattels, to go in succession, or to take place after the death of the seller or donor, or to or for such support, use or benefit—and also every devise of goods or chattels to or for the support, use or benefit of any minister, public teacher, or preacher of the gospel, as such, or any religious sect, order, or denomination, without the leave of the Legislature, shall be void; except always any sale, gift, lease or devise of any quantity of land, not exceeding two acres, for a church, meeting, or other house of worship, and for a burying-ground, which shall be improved, enjoyed or used only for such purpose—or such sale, gift, lease, or devise, shall be void.

XXXV.   That no other test or qualification ought to be required, on admission to any office of trust or profit, than such oath of support and fidelity to this State, and such oath of office, as shall be directed by this convention, or the Legislature of this State, and a declaration of a belief in the Christian religion.

XXXVI.   That the manner of administering an oath to any person, ought to be such, as those of the religious persuasion, profession, or denomination, of which such person is one, generally esteem the most effectual confirmation, by the attestation of the Divine Being.   And that the people called Quakers, those called Dunkers, and those called Menonists, holding it unlawful to take an oath on any occasion, ought to be allowed to make their solemn affirmation, in the manner that Quakers have been allowed and accepted within this State, instead of an oath.   And further, on such affirmation, warrants to search for stolen goods, or for the apprehension of commitment of offenders, ought to be granted, or security for the peace awarded, and Quakers, Dunkers or Menonists ought also, on their solemn affirmation as aforesaid, to be admitted as witnesses, in all criminal cases not capital.

IV.   CONNECTICUT

34.   Constitution of Connecticut, 1776.

Poore, 257.

The People of this State, being by the Providence of God, free and independent, have the sole and exclusive Right of governing themselves as a free, sovereign, and independent State; and having from their Ancestors derived a free and excellent Constitution of Government whereby the Legislature depends on the free and annual Election of the People, they have the best

Security for the Preservation of their civil and religious Rights and Liberties. And forasmuch as the free Fruition of such Liberties and Privileges as Humanity, Civility and Christianity call for, as is due to every man in his Place and Proportion, without Impeachment and Infringement, hath ever been, and will be the Tranquility and Stability of Churches and Commonwealths; and the Denial thereof, the Disturbance, if not the Ruin of both.

VI.   NORTH CAROLINA

35.   Constitution of North Carolina, 1776.

Poore, 1410, 1413.

XIX.   That all men have a natural and unalienable right to worship Almighty God according to the dictates of their own consciences.

XXXI.   That no clergyman, or preacher of the gospel, of any denomination, shall be capable of being a member of either the Senate, House of Commons, or Council of State, while he continues in the exercise of the pastoral function.

XXXII.   That no person, who shall deny the being of God or the truth of the Protestant religion, or the divine authority either of the Old or New Testaments, or who shall hold religious principles incompatible with the freedom and safety of the State, shall be capable of holding any office or place of trust or profit in the civil department within this State.

XXXIV.   That there shall be no establishment of any one religious church or denomination in this State, in preference to any other; neither shall any person, on any pretence whatsoever, be compelled to attend any place of worship contrary to his own faith or judgment, nor be obliged to pay, for the purchase of any glebe, or the building of any house of worship, or for the maintenance of any minister or ministry, contrary to what he believes right, or has voluntarily and personally engaged to perform; but all persons shall be at liberty to exercise their own mode of worship:—*Provided,* That nothing herein contained shall be construed to exempt preachers of treasonable or seditious discourses, from legal trial and punishment.

VII. SOUTH CAROLINA

36. Constitution of South Carolina, 1778.

Poore, 1621, 1622, 1623.

Governor and Lieutenant-Governor and privy council, all of the Protestant religion.
Members of legislature of Protestant religion.

XXI. And whereas the ministers of the gospel are by their profession dedicated to the service of God and the cure of souls, and ought not to be diverted from the great duties of their function, therefore no minister of the gospel or public preacher of any religious persuasion, while he continues in the exercise of his pastoral function, and for two years after, shall be eligible either as governor, lieutenant-governor, a member of the senate, house of representatives, or privy council in this State.

XXXVIII. That all persons and religious societies who acknowledge that there is one God, and a future state of rewards and punishments, and that God is publicly to be worshipped, shall be freely tolerated. The Christian Protestant religion shall be deemed, and is hereby constituted and declared to be, the established religion of this State. That all denominations of Christian Protestants in this State, demeaning themselves peaceably and faithfully, shall enjoy equal religious and civil privileges. To accomplish this desirable purpose without injury to the religious property of those societies of Christians which are by law already incorporated for the purpose of religious worship, and to put it fully into the power of every other society of Christian Protestants, either already formed or hereafter to be formed, to obtain the like incorporation, it is hereby constituted, appointed, and declared that the respective societies of the Church of England that are already formed in this State for the purpose of religious worship shall still continue incorporate and hold the religious property now in their possession. And that whenever fifteen or more male persons, not under twenty-one years of age, professing the Christian Protestant religion, and agreeing to unite themselves in a society for the purposes of religious worship, they shall, (on complying with the terms hereinafter mentioned,) be, and be constituted, a church, and be esteemed and regarded in law as of the established religion of the State, and on a petition to the legislature shall be entitled to be incorporated and to enjoy equal privileges, That every society of Christians so formed shall give themselves a name or denomination by which they shall be called and known in law, and all that associate with them for the purposes of worship shall be esteemed as belonging to the society so called. But that previous to the establishment and incorporation of the respective societies of every denomination as aforesaid, and in order to entitle them thereto, each society so petitioning shall have agreed to and subscribed in a book the following five articles, without which no agreement or union of men upon pretence of religion shall entitle them to be incorporated and esteemed as a church of the established religion of this State:

1st. That there is one eternal God, and a future state of rewards and punishments.

2d. That God is publicly to be worshipped.

3d. That the Christian religion is the true religion.

4th. That the holy scriptures of the Old and New Testaments are of divine inspiration, and are the rule of faith and practice.

5th. That it is lawful and the duty of every man being thereunto called by those that govern, to bear witness to the truth.

And that every inhabitant of this State, when called to make an appeal to God as a witness of truth, shall be permitted to do it in that way which is most agreeable to the dictates of his own conscience. And that the people of this State may forever enjoy the right of electing their own pastors or clergy, and at the same time that the State may have sufficient security for the due discharge of the pastoral office, by those who shall be admitted to be clergymen, no person shall officiate as minister of any established church who shall not have been chosen by a majority of the society to which he shall minister, or by persons appointed by the said majority, to choose and procure a minister for them; nor until the minister so chosen and appointed shall have made and subscribed to the following declaration, over and above the aforesaid five articles, viz: "That he is determined by God's grace out of the holy scriptures, to instruct the people committed to his charge, and to teach nothing as required of necessity to eternal salvation but that which he shall be persuaded may be concluded and proved from the scripture; that he will use both public and private admonitions, as well to the sick as to the whole within his cure, as need shall require and occasion shall be given, and that he will be diligent in prayers, and in reading of the holy scriptures, and in such studies as help to the knowledge of the same; that he will be diligent to frame and fashion his own self and his family according to the doctrine of Christ, and to make both himself and them, as much as in him lieth, wholesome examples and patterns to the flock of Christ; that he will maintain and set forward, as much as he can, quietness, peace, and love among all people, and especially among those that are or shall be committed to his charge. No person shall disturb or molest any religious assembly; nor shall use any reproachful, reviling, or abusive language against any church, that being the certain way of disturbing the peace, and of hindering the conversion of any to the truth, by engaging them in quarrels and animosities, to the hatred of the professors, and that profession which otherwise they might be brought to assent to. No person whatsoever shall speak anything in their religious assembly irreverently or seditiously of the government of this State. No person shall, by law, be obliged to pay towards the maintenance and support of a religious worship that he does not freely join in, or has not voluntarily engaged to support. But the churches, chapels, parsonages, glebes, and all other property now belonging to any societies of the Church of England, or any other religious socieites, shall remain and be secured to them forever. The poor shall be supported, and elections managed in the accustomed manner, until laws shall be provided to adjust those matters in the most equitable way.

37. Constitution of South Carolina, 1790.

Poore, 1630.

Section 23 similar to XXI of 1778.

Section I. The free exercise and enjoyment of religious profession and worship, without discrimination or preference, shall forever hereafter be allowed within this State to all mankind: *Provided,* That the liberty of conscience thereby declared shall not be so construed as to excuse acts of licentiousness, or justify practices inconsistent with the peace or safety of this State.

Section 2. The rights, privileges, immunities, and estates

of both civil and religious societies, and of corporate bodies, shall remain as if the constitution of this State had not been altered or amended.

VIII.   NEW JERSEY

38.   Constitution of New Jersey, 1776.

Poore, 1313.

XVIII.   That no person shall ever, within this Colony, be deprived of the inestimable privilege of worshipping Almighty God in a manner agreeable to the dictates of his own conscience; nor, under any pretence whatever, be compelled to attend any place of worship, contrary to his own faith and judgment; nor shall any person, within this Colony, ever be obliged to pay tithes, taxes, or any other rates, for the purpose of building or repairing any other church or churches, place or places of worship, or for the maintenance of any minister or ministry, contrary to what he believes to be right, or has deliberately or voluntarily engaged himself to perform.

XIX.   That there shall be no establishment of any one religious sect in this Province, in preference to another; and that no Protestant inhabitant of this Colony shall be denied the enjoyment of any civil right, merely on account of his religious principles; but that all persons, professing a belief in the faith of any Protestant sect, who shall demean themselves peaceably under the government, as hereby established, shall be capable of being elected into any office of profit or trust, or being a member of either branch of the Legislature, and shall fully and freely enjoy every privilege and immunity, enjoyed by others of their fellow subjects.

IX.   NEW YORK

39.   Constitution of New York, 1777.

Poore, 1328.

XXXVIII.   And whereas we are required, by the benevolent principles of rational liberty, not only to expel civil tyranny, but also to guard against that spiritual oppression and intolerance wherewith the bigotry and ambition of weak and wicked priests and princes have scourged mankind, this convention doth further, in the name and by the authority of the good people of this State, ordain, determine, and declare, that the free exercise and enjoyment of religious profession and worship, without discrimination or preference, shall forever hereafter be allowed, within this State, to all mankind: *Provided,* That the liberty of conscience, hereby granted, shall not be so construed as to excuse acts of licentiousness, or justify practices inconsistent with the peace or safety of this State.

XXXIX. And whereas the ministers of the gospel are, by their profession, dedicated to the service of God and the care of souls, and ought not to be diverted from the great duties of their function; therefore, no minister of the gospel, or priest of any denomination whatsoever, shall, at any time hereafter, under any pretence or description whatever, be eligible to, or capable of holding, any civil or military office or place within this State.

XL. And whereas it is of the utmost importance to the safety of every State that it should always be in a condition of defence; and it is the duty of every man who enjoys the protection of society to be prepared and willing to defend it; this convention therefore, in the name and by the authority of the good people of this State, doth ordain, determine, and declare that the militia of this State, at all times hereafter, as well in peace as in war, shall be armed and disciplined, and in readiness for service. That all such of the inhabitants of this State being of the people called Quakers as, from scruples of conscience, may be averse to the bearing of arms, be therefrom excused by the legislature; and do pay to the State such sums of money, in lieu of their personal service, as the same may, in the judgment of the legislature, be worth. And that a proper magazine of warlike stores, proportionate to the number of inhabitants, be, forever hereafter, at the expense of this State, and by acts of the legislature, established, maintained, and continued in every county in this State.

XXLII. And this convention doth further, in the name and by the authority of the good people of this State, ordain, determine, and declare that it shall be in the discretion of the legislature to naturalize all such persons, and in such manner, as they shall think proper: *Provided,* All such of the persons so to be by them naturalized, as being born in parts beyond sea, and out of the United States of America, shall come to settle in and become subjects of this State, shall take an oath of allegiance to ths State, and abjure and renounce all allegiance and subjection to all and every foreign king, prince, potentate, and State in all matters, ecclesiastical as well as civil.

X.   NEW HAMPSHIRE

40.   Constitution of New Hampshire, 1784.

Poore, 1280.

ARTICLE I

IV.   Among the natural rights some are in their very nature unalienable, because no equivalent can be given or received for them.   Of this kind are the *Rights of Conscience*.

V.   Every individual has a natural and unalienable right to worship God according to the dictates of his own conscience and reason; and no subject shall be hurt, molested, or restrained, in his person, liberty, or estate, for worshipping God in the manner and season most agreeable to the dictates of his own conscience, or for his religious profession, sentiments or persuasion, provided he doth not disturb the public peace or disturb others in their religious worship.

VI.   As morality and piety, rightly grounded on evangelical principles, will give the best and greatest security to government, and will lay in the hearts of men the strongest obligations to due subjection, and as the knowledge of these is most likely to be propagated through a society by the institution of the public worship of the Deity and of public instruction in morality and religion, therefore, to promote these important purposes, the people of this state have a right to empower, and do hereby fully empower, the Legislature to authorize, from time to time, the several towns, parishes, bodies corporate or religious societies within this state to make adequate provision at their own expense, for the support and maintenance of public Protestant teachers of piety, religion, and morality.   Provided, notwithstanding, that the several towns, parishes, bodies corporate or religious societies shall at all times have the exclusive right of electing their own public teachers, and of contracting with them for their support and maintenance. And no person of any one particular religious sect or denomination shall ever be compelled to pay towards the support of the teacher or teachers of another persuasion, sect, or denomination. And of every denomination of Christians, demeaning themselves quietly, and as good subjects of the state, shall be equally under the protection of the law, and no subordination of any one sect or denomination to another shall ever be established by law. And nothing herein shall be understood to affect any former contracts made for the support of the ministry, but all such contracts shall remain and be in the same state as if this constitution had not been made. No person who is conscientiously scrupulous about the lawfulness of bearing arms shall be compelled to do thereto, provided he will pay an equivalent.

XI. PENNSYLVANIA

41. Constitution of Pennsylvania, 1776.

Poore, 1541.

II. That all men have a natural and unalienable right to worship Almighty God according to the dictates of their own consciences and understanding: And that no man ought or of right can be compelled to attend any religious worship, or erect or support any place of worship, or maintain any ministry, contrary to, or against, his own free will and consent: Nor can any man, who acknowleges the being of a God, be justly deprived or abridged of any civil right as a citizen, on account of his religious sentiments or peculiar mode of religious worship: And that no authority can or ought to be vested in, or assumed by any power whatever, that shall in any case interfere with, or in any manner controul, the right of conscience in the free exercise of religious worship.

Sect. 45. Laws for the enforcement of virtue, and prevention of vice and immorality shall be made and constantly kept in force, and provision shall be made for their due execution: And all religious societies or bodies of men heretofore united or incorporated for the advancement of religion or learning, or for other pious and charitable purposes, shall be encouraged and protected in the enjoyment of the privileges, immunities and estates which they were accustomed to enjoy, or could of right have enjoyed, under the laws and former constitution of this state.

42.   Constitution of Pennsylvania, 1790.

Poore, 1554.

ARTICLE IX

Sec. 3.   That all men have a natural and indefeasible right to worship Almighty God according to the dictates of their own consciences; that no man can of right be compelled to attend, erect, or support any place of worship, or to maintain any ministry, against his consent; that no human authority can, in any case whatever, control or interfere with the rights of conscience; and that no preference shall ever be given, by law, to any religious establishments or modes of worship.

Sec. 4.   That no person, who acknowledges the being of a God and a future state of rewards and punishments, shall, on account of his religious sentiments, be disqualified to hold any office or place of trust or profit under this commonwealth.

XII.   DELAWARE

43.   Constitution of Delaware, 1776.

Poore, 276.

ART. 22.   Every person who shall be chosen a member of either house, or appointed to any office or place of trust, before taking his seat, or entering upon the execution of his office, shall take the following oath, or affirmation, if conscientiously scrupulous of taking an oath, to wit:

"I, A B, will bear true allegiance to the Delaware State, submit to its constitution and laws, and do no act wittingly whereby the freedom thereof may be prejudiced."

And also make and subscribe the following declaration, to wit:

"I, A B, do profess faith in God the Father, and Jesus Christ His only Son, and in the Holy Ghost, one God, blessed for evermore; and I do acknowledge the holy scriptures of the Old and New Testament to be given by divine inspiration."

And all officers shall also take an oath of office.

ART. 29.   There shall be no establishment of any one religious sect in this State in preference to another; and no clergyman or preacher of the gospel, of any denomination, shall be capable of holding any civil office in this State, or of being a member of either of the branches of the legislature, while they continue in the exercise of the pastoral function.

XIII.   GEORGIA

44.   Constitution of Georgia, 1777.

Poore, 383.

Art. LVI.   All persons whatever shall have the free exercise of their religion; provided it be not repugnant to the peace and safety of the State; and shall not, unless by consent, support any teacher or teachers except those of their own profession.

45.   Constitution of Georgia, 1789.

Poore, 386.

ARTICLE IV

Sec. 5.   All persons shall have the free exercise of religion, without being obliged to contribute to the support of any religious profession but their own.

THE UNITED STATES

46.   In Congress, July 13, 1787, an ordinance for the Government of the Territory of the United States northwest of the Ohio River.

ARTICLE I.   No person, demeaning himself in a peaceful and orderly manner, shall ever be molested on account of his mode of worship or religious sentiments, in the said Territory.

ARTICLE III.   Religion, morality, and knowledge, being necessary to good government and the happiness of mankind, schools and the means of education shall forever be encouraged. The utmost good faith shall always be observed towards the Indians: their lands and property shall never be taken from them without their consent, and in their property, rights, and liberty they shall never be invaded or disturbed, unless in just and lawful wars authorized by Congress, but laws founded in justice and humanity shall from time to time, be made for preventing wrongs being done to them, and for preserving peace and friendship with them.

ARTICLE VI.   There shall be neither slavery nor involuntary servitude in the said Territory, otherwise than in the punishment of crimes, whereof the party shall have been duly convicted: Provided always, that any person escaping into the same, from whom labor or service is lawfully claimed in any one of the original States, such fugitive may be lawfully reclaimed, and conveyed to the person claiming his or her labor or service as aforesaid.   Be it ordained by the authority aforesaid, that the resolutions of the 23rd of April, 1784, relative to the subject of this ordinance, be, and the same are hereby repealed and declared null and void.

47.   ARTICLE VI, 1787.

. . . but no religious test shall ever be required as a qualification to any office or public trust under the United States.

48.   Amendment I, 1791.

Congress shall make no law respecting an establishment of religion, or prohibiting the free exercise thereof; . . .

49.   Amendment V, 1791.

. . . nor be deprived of life, liberty, or property, without due process of law.

XIV.   VERMONT, 1791

50.   Constitution of 1777.

Poore, 1857.

CHAPTER I

III.   That all men have a natural and unalienable right to worship Almighty God, according to the dictates of their own consciences and understandings, as in their opinion shall be regulated by the word of God; and that no man ought to, or of right can be compelled to attend any religious worship or erect or support any place of worship, or to maintain any minister, contrary to the dictates of his conscience, nor can any man be justly deprived or abridged of any civil right as a citizen, on account of his religious sentiments, or peculiar mode of worship; and that no authority can, or ought to be vested in, or assumed by, any power whatever, that shall in any case interfere with, or in any manner control the rights of conscience, in the free exercise of religious worship. Nevertheless, every sect or denomination of Christians ought to observe the sabbath or Lord's Day, and keep up some sort of religious worship, which to them shall seem most agreeable to the revealed will of God.

IX. . . . nor can any man who is conscientiously scrupulous of bearing arms, be justly compelled thereto, if he will pay an equivalent, . . .

CHAPTER II

Sec. IX. And each member before he takes his seat, shall make and subscribe the following declaration, viz:

I do believe in one God, the Creator and Governor of the universe, the rewarder of the good and punisher of the wicked. And I do acknowledge the scriptures of the old and new testament to be given by divine inspiration, and own and profess the protestant religion.

And no further or other religious test shall ever, hereafter, be required of any civil officer of magistrate in this State.

51. Constitution of 1786 repeats religious sections.

C

RELIGIOUS REFERENCES IN STATE CONSTITUTIONS, A. D., 1791-1837

III. MARYLAND

52. Amendments to Constitution of 1776, ratified 1792.
Poore, 829.

ART. III.   That every person being a member of either of the religious sects or societies called Quakers, Menonists, Tunkers, or Nicolites, or New Quakers, and who shall be conscientiously scrupulous of taking an oath on any occasion, being otherwise qualified and duly elected a senator, delegate, or elector of the senate, or being otherwise qualified and duly appointed or elected to any office of profit or trust, on making affirmation instead of taking the several oaths appointed by the constitution and form of government, and the several acts of this State now in force, or that hereafter may be made, such persons may hold and exercise any office of profit or trust to which he may be appointed or elected, and may, by such affirmation, qualify himself to take a seat in the legislature, and to act therein as a member of the same in all cases whatsoever, or to be an elector of the senate, in as full and ample a manner, to all intents and purposes whatever, as persons are now competent and qualified to act who are not conscientiously scrupulous of taking such oaths.

ART. V. Section I.   That the people called Quakers, those called Nicolites, or New Quakers, those called Tunkers, and those called Menonists, holding it unlawful to take an oath on any occasion, shall be allowed to make their solemn affirmation as witnesses, in the manner that Quakers have been heretofore allowed to affirm, which affirmation shall be of the same avail as an oath, to all intents and purposes whatever.

X.   NEW HAMPSHIRE

53.   Constitution of New Hampshire, 1792.
No change in religious articles.

XII.   DELAWARE

54.   Constitution of Delaware, 1792.

Poore, 278.

We, the people, hereby ordain and establish this constitution of government for the State of Delaware.

Through divine goodness all men have, by nature, the rights of worshipping and serving their Creator according to the dictates of their consciences, of enjoying and defending life and liberty, of acquiring and protecting reputation and property, and, in general, of attaining objects suitable to their condition, without injury by one to another; and as these rights are essential to their welfare, for the due exercise thereof, power is inherent in them; and, therefore, all just authority in the institutions of political society is derived from the people, and established with their consent, to advance their happiness; and they may, for this end, as circumstances require, from time to time, alter their constitution of government.

ARTICLE I

Sec. 1.   Although it is the duty of all men frequently to assemble together for the public worship of Almighty God; and for piety and morality, on which the prosperity of the communities depend, are hereby promoted: yet no man shall or ought to be compelled to attend any religious worship, or to the maintenance of any ministry, against his own free will and consent: and no power shall or ought to be vested in or assumed by any magistrate that shall in any case interfere with, or in any manner control the rights of conscience, in the free exercise of religious worship, nor a preference given by law to any religious societies, denominations, or modes of worship.

Sec. 2.   No religious test shall be required as a qualification to any office or public trust, under this State.

XIV.   VERMONT

55.   Constitution of Vermont, 1793 repeats religious sections of 1786 except chapter II, Sec. 1.

XV.   KENTUCKY, 1792.

56.   Constitution of 1792.
Poore, 654.

ARTICLE XII

That all men have a natural and indefeasible right to worship Almighty God according to the dictates of their own consciences; no man of right can be compelled to attend, erect or support any place of worship, or to maintain any ministry against his consent; that no human authority can in any case whatever control or interfere with the rights of conscience; and that no preference shall ever be given by law to any religious societies or modes of worship.

That the civil rights, privileges or capacities of any citizen shall in no way be diminished or enlarged on account of his religion.

57.   Constitution of 1709.   Poore, 666.
Article X. sec. 3 and 4, as above.

XVI.   TENNESSEE, 1796.

58.   Constitution of 1796.
Poore, 1672.

ARTICLE VIII

Sec. I.   Whereas ministers of the gospel are, by their professions, dedicated to God and the care of souls, and ought not be diverted from the great duties of their functions; therefore no minister of the gospel, or priest of any denomination whatever, shall be eligible to a seat in either house of the Legislature.

Sec. 2.   No person who denies the being of God, or a future state of rewards and punishments, shall hold any office in the civil department of this State.

ARTICLE XI.

Sec. 3.   That all men have a natural and indefeasible right to worship Almighty God according to the dictates of their own conscience; that no man can, of right, be compelled to attend, erect, or support any place of worship, or to maintain any minister, against his consent; that no human authority can, in any case whatever, control or interfere with the rights of conscience; and that no preference shall ever be given, by law, to any religious establishment or mode of worship.

Sec. 4. That no political or religious test shall ever be required as a qualification to any office or public trust under this State.

59. Constitution of 1834.

Article I, Sec. 3 and 4 same as 1796, XI, 3, 4.

Article IX, Sec. 1 and 2 same as 1796, VIII, 1, 2.

XVII. OHIO, 1803

60. Constitution of 1802.

Poore, 1461.

ARTICLE VIII

Sec. 3. That all men have a natural and indefeasible right to worship Almighty God according to the dictates of their conscience; that no human authority can, in any case whatever, control or interfere with the rights of conscience; that no man shall be compelled to attend, erect, or support any place of worship, or to maintain any ministry, against his consent; and that no preference shall ever be given by law to any religious society or mode of worship; and no religious test shall be required as a qualification to any office of trust or profit. But religion, morality, and knowledge being essentially necessary to the good government and the happiness of mankind, schools and the means of instruction shall forever be encouraged by legislative provision, not inconsistent with the rights of conscience.

Sec. 26. The laws shall be passed by the legislature which shall secure to each and every denomination of religious societies in each surveyed township, which now is or may hereafter be formed in the State, an equal participation, according to their number of adherents, of the profits arising from the land granted by Congress for the support of religion, agreeably to the ordinance or act of Congress making the appropriation.

XVIII. LOUISIANA, 1812.

61. Constitution of 1812.
Poore, 702.

ARTICLE II

Sec. 22. No person, while he continues to exercise the functions of a clergyman, priest, or teacher of any religious persuasion, society or sect, shall be eligible to the general assembly or to any office of profit or trust under this State.

XIX. INDIANA, 1816.

62. Constitution of 1816.
Poore, 500.

ARTICLE I

Sec. 3. That all men have a natural and indefeasible right to worship Almighty God according to the dictates of their own consciences; that no man shall be compelled to attend, erect, or support any place of worship, or to maintain any ministry, against his consent; that no human authority can, in any case whatever, control or interfere with the rights of conscience; and that no preference shall ever be given by law to any religious societies or modes of worship; and no religious test shall be required as a qualification to any office of trust or profit.

ARTICLE VII

Sec. 2. No person or persons, conscientiously scrupulous of bearing arms, shall be compelled to do militia duty: *Provided,* Such person or persons shall pay an equivalent for such exemption; which equivalent shall be collected annually, by a civil officer, and be hereafter fixed by law; and shall be equal, as near as may be, to the lowest fines assessed on those privates in militia who may neglect or refuse to perform military duty.

ARTICLE XI

Sec. 4. The manner of administering an oath or affirmation shall be such as is most consistent with the conscience of the deponent, and shall be esteemed the most solemn appeal to God.

XX. MISSISSIPPI, 1817.

63. Constitution of 1817.

Poore, 1055.

ARTICLE I

Sec. 3. The exercise and enjoyment of religious profession and worship, without discrimination, shall forever be free to all persons in this State: *Provided,* That the right hereby declared and established shall not be so construed as to excuse acts of licentiousness, or justify practices inconsistent with the peace and safety of this State.

Sec. 4. No preference shall ever be given by law to any religious sect or mode of worship.

Sec. 5. That no person shall be molested for his opinions on any subject whatever, nor suffer any civil or political incapacity, or acquire any civil or political advantage, in consequence of such opinions, except in cases provided for in this constitution.

ARTICLE IV, Section 25.

Sec. 3. Those persons who conscientiously scruple to bear arms shall not be compelled to do so, but shall pay an equivalent for personal service.

ARTICLE VI.

Sec. 6. No person who denies the being of God or a future state of rewards and punishments shall hold any office in the civil department of this State.

Sec. 7. Ministers of the gospel being, by their profession, dedicated to God and the care of souls, ought not to be diverted from the great duties of their functions; therefore, no minister of the gospel, or priest of any denomination whatever, shall be eligible to the office of governor, lieutenant-governor, or to a seat in either branch of the general assembly.

Sec. 16. Religion, morality, and knowledge being necessary to good government, the preservation of liberty, and the happiness of mankind, schools, and the means of education, shall forever be encouraged in this State.

64.   Constitution of 1832.
Poore, 1067.

ARTICLE I

Sec. 3 as Constitution 1817, I, 3
Sec. 4 as Constitution 1817, I, 4
Sec. 5 as Constitution 1817, I, 5.

ARTICLE VII

Sec. 5 as VI, 6, 1817
Sec. 14 as VI, 16, 1817

XXI.   ILLINOIS, 1818

65.   Constitution of 1818.
Poore, 445.

ARTICLE V

Sec. 2.   No person or persons conscientiously scrupulous of bearing arms shall be compelled to do militia duty in time of peace: *Provided,* Such person or persons shall pay an equivalent for such exemptions.

ARTICLE VIII

Sec. 3.   That all men have a natural and indefeasible right to worship Almighty God according to the dictates of their own consciences; that no man can of right be compelled to attend, erect, or support any place of worship, or to maintain any ministry against his consent; that no human authority can, in any case whatever, control or interfere with the rights of conscience; and that no preference shall ever be given by law to any religious establishments or modes of worship.

Sec. 4.   That no religious test shall ever be required as a qualification to any office or public trust under this State.

IV. CONNECTICUT

66. Constitution of 1818.

Poore, 258.

Preamble. The people of Connecticut acknowledging with gratitude, the good providence of God, . . .

Article I. Declaration of Rights.

Sec. 3. The exercise and enjoyment of religious profession and worship, without discrimination, shall forever be free to all persons in this State, provided that the right hereby declared and established, shall not be construed as to excuse acts of licentiousness, or to justify practices inconsistent with the peace and safety of the State.

Sec. 4. No preference shall be given by law to any Christian sect or mode of worship.

Sec. 5. Every citizen may freely speak, write and publish his sentiments on all subjects, being responsible for the abuse of that liberty.

Article VII of Religion

Sec. 1. It being the duty of all men to worship the Supreme Being, the Great Creator and Preserver of the Universe, and their right to render that worship, in the mode most consistent with the dictates of their consciousness, no person shall by law be compelled to join or support, nor be classed with, or associated to, any congregation, church or religious association. But every person now belonging to such congregation, church or religious association shall remain a member thereof until he shall have separated himself therefrom, in the manner hereinafter provided. And each and every society or denomination of Christians in this State, shall have and enjoy the same and equal powers, rights and privileges; and shall have power and authority to support and maintain the ministers or teachers of their respective denominations, and to build and repair houses for public worship, by a tax on the members of any such society only, to be laid by a major vote of the legal voters assembled at any society meeting, warned and held according to law, or in any other manner.

Sec. 2. If any person shall choose to separate himself

from the society or denomination of Christians to which he may belong, and shall leave written notice thereof with the clerk of such society, he shall there upon be no longer liable for any future expenses which may be incurred by said society.

XXII.   ALABAMA, 1819

67. Constitution of 1819.
Poore, 33.

ARTICLE I

Sec. 3.   No person within this State shall, upon any pretence, be deprived of the inestimable privilege of worshipping God in the manner most agreeable to his own conscience; nor be compelled to attend any place of worship; nor shall any one ever be obliged to pay tithes, taxes, or other rate, for the building or repairing any place of worship, or for the maintenance of any minister or ministry.

Sec. 4.   No human authority ought, in case whatever, to control or interfere with the rights of conscience.

Sec. 5.   No person shall be hurt, molested, or restrained in his religious profession, sentiments, or persuasions, provided he does not disturb others in their religious worship.

Sec. 6.   The civil rights, privileges, or capacities of any citizen, shall in no way be diminished or enlarged, on account of his religious principles.

Sec. 7.   There shall be no establishment of religion by law; no preference shall ever be given by law to any religious sect, society, denomination or mode of worship; or public trust under this state.

ARTICLE IV, Section 24

Sec. 2.   Any person, who conscientiously scruples to bear arms, shall not be compelled to do so, but shall pay an equivalent for personal service.

XXIII.   MAINE, 1820.

68. Constitution of 1820.
Poore, 788.
Preamble: .... acknowledging with grateful hearts the goodness

of the Sovereign Ruler of the Universe in affording us an opportunity, so favorable to the design; and, imploring His aid and direction in it accomplishment, . . .

Sec. 3. All men have a natural and unalienable right to worship Almighty God according to the dictates of their own consciences, and no one shall be hurt, molested, or restrained in his person, liberty or estate for worshipping God in the manner and season most agreeable to the dictates of his conscience, nor for his religious professions or sentiments, provided he does not disturb the public peace, nor obstruct others in their religious worship; and all persons demeaning themselves peaceably, as good members of the State, shall be equally under the protection of the laws, and no subordination nor preference of any office or trust under this State; and all religious societies in this State, whether incorporate or unincorporate, shall at all time have the exclusive right of electing their public teachers, and contracting with them for their support and maintenance.

ARTICLE VII

Sec. 5. Persons of the denomination of Quakers and Shakers, justices of the Supreme Judicial court and ministers of the gospel may be exempted from military duty, but no other person of the age of eighteen and under the age of forty-five years, excepting officers of the militia who have been honorably discharged, shall be so exempted, unless he shall pay an equivalent to be fixed by law.

ARTICLE IX

Sec. 1. *Provided,* That an affirmation in the above forms may be substituted, when the persons shall be conscientiously scrupulous of taking and subscribing to an oath.

XXIV. MISSOURI, 1821

69. Constitution of 1820.

Poore, 1106.

ARTICLE III

Sec. 13. No person while he continues to exercise the

functions of a bishop, priest, clergyman, or teacher of any religious persuasion, denomination, society, or sect whatsoever, shall be eligible to either house of the general assembly; nor shall he be appointed to any office of profit within the State, the office of justice of the peace excepted.

ARTICLE XIII

Sec. 4.   That all men have a natural and indefeasible right to worship Almighty God according to the dictates of their own consciences; that no man can be compelled to erect, support, or attend any place of worship, or to maintain any minister of the gospel or teacher of religion; that no human authority can control or interfere with the rights of conscience; that no person can ever be hurt, molested, or restrained in his religious profession or sentiments, if he do not disturb others in their religious worship.

Sec. 5.   That no person on account of his religious opinions, can be rendered ineligible to any office of trust or profit under this State; that no preference can ever be given by law to any sect or mode of worship; and that no religious corporation can ever be established in this State.

Sec. 18.   That no person who is religiously scrupulous of bearing arms can be compelled to do so, but may be compelled to pay an equivalent for military service, in such manner as shall be prescribed by law; and that no priest, preacher of the gospel, or teacher of any religious persuasion or sect, regularly ordained as such, be subject to militia duty, or compelled to bear arms.

IX.   NEW YORK

70.   Constitution of 1821.

Poore, 1341.

We, the people of the State of New York, acknowledging with gratitude the grace and beneficence of God in permitting us to make choice of our form of government, do establish this constitution.

ARTICLE VI.

Members of the legislature and all officers, executive and judicial, except such inferior officers as may by law be exempted, shall, before they enter on the duties of their respective offices, take and subscribe the following oath or affirmation:

"I do solemnly swear [or affirm, as the case may be] that I will support the Constitution of the United States, and the constitution of the State of New York; and that I will faithfully discharge the duties of the office of —————— according to the best of my ability."

And no other oath, declaration, or test shall be required as a qualification for any office or public trust.

ARTICLE VII.

Sec. 3.   The free exercise and enjoyment of religious profession and worship, without discrimination or preference, shall forever be allowed in this State to all mankind; but the liberty of conscience hereby secured shall not be so construed as to excuse acts of licentiousness, or justify practices inconsistent with peace or safety of this State.

Sec. 4.   Same as XXXIX of Constitution, 1777.

Sec. 5.   The militia of this State shall at all times hereafter be armed and disciplined and in readiness for service; but all such inhabitants of this State, of any religious denomination whatever, as from scruples of conscience may be averse to bearing arms, shall be excused therefrom by paying to the State an equivalent in money; and the legislature shall provide by law for the collection of such equivalent, to be estimated according to the expense, in time and money, of an ordinary able-bodied militia-man.

II.   MASSACHUSETTS

71.   Amendments to Constitution of 1780.

Poore, 973.

(1)   Ratified 1822.

ART. VI.   Instead of the oath of allegiance prescribed by the constitution, the following oath shall be taken and subscribed by every person chosen or appointed to any office, civil or military, under the government of this commonwealth, before he shall enter on the duties of his office, to wit:—

"I, A. B., do solemnly swear, that I will bear true faith and allegiance to the Commonwealth of Massachusetts, and will support the constitution thereof.   So help me, God."

Provided, That when any person shall be of the denomination called Quakers, and shall decline taking said oath, he shall make his affirmation in the foregoing form, omitting the word "swear" and inserting, instead thereof, the word "affirm," and omitting the words "So help me, God," and subjoining instead thereof, the words, "This I do under the pains and penalties of perjury."

(2)   Ratified 1833.

ART. XI.   Instead of the third article of the bill of rights, the following modification and amendment thereof is substituted:—

As the public worship of God and instructions in piety, religion, and morality, promote the happiness and prosperity of a people, and the security of a republican government; therefore, the several religious societies of this commonwealth, whether corporate or unincorporate, at any meeting legally warned and holden for that purpose, shall ever have the right to elect their pastors or religious teachers, to contract with them for their support, to raise money for erecting and repairing houses for public worship, for the maintenance of religious instruction, and for payment of necessary expenses; and all persons belonging to any religious society shall be taken and held to be members, until they shall file with the clerk of such a society a written notice, declaring the dissolution of their membership, and thenceforth shall not be liable for any grant or contract which may be thereafter made, or entered into by such society; and all religious sects and denominations, demeaning themselves peaceably, and as good citizens of the commonwealth, shall be equally under the protection of the law; and no subordination of any one sect or denomination to another shall ever be established by law.

XII.   DELAWARE

72.   Constitution of 1831.
Poore, 289.

(1)   Preamble

We, the people, hereby ordain and establish this constitution of government for the State of Delaware.

Through divine goodness all men have, by nature, the rights of worshipping and serving their Creator according to the dictates of their consciences; of enjoying and defending life and liberty, of acquiring and protecting reputation and property, and, in general, of attaining objects suitable to their condition, without injury by one to another; and as these rights are essential to their welfare, for the due exercise thereof, power is inherent in them; and therefore all just authority in the institutions of political happiness. And they may for this end, as circumstances require, from time to time, alter their constitution of government.

ARTICLE I.

SECTION 1. Although it is the duty of all men frequently to assemble together for the public worship of the Author of the universe, and piety and morality, on which the prosperity of communities depends, are thereby promoted, yet no man shall, or ought to be compelled to attend any religious worship, to contribute to the erection or support of any place of worship, or to the maintenance of any ministry, against his own free will and consent; and no power shall or ought to be vested in or assumed by any magistrate that shall, in any case, interfere with, or in any manner control, the rights of conscience in the free exercise of religious worship; nor shall a preference be given by law to any religious societies, denomination, or modes of worship.

SEC. 2. No religious test shall be required as a qualification to any office or public trust under this State.

VI. NORTH CAROLINA

73. Amendment Ratified 1835.

Poore, 1418.

ART. IV, Sec. 2. The thirty-second section of the constitution shall be amended to read as follows: No person who shall deny the being of God, or the truth of the Christian religion, or the divine authority of the Old or New Testament, or who shall hold religious principles incompatible with the freedom or safety of the State, shall be capable of holding any office or place of trust or profit in the civil department within this State.

XXV.   ARKANSAS, 1836

74. Constitution of 1836.
Poore, 102.

ARTICLE II.

Sec. 3.   That all men have a natural and indefeasible right to worship Almighty God according to the dictates of their own consciences; and no man can of right be compelled to attend, erect or support any place of worship, or to maintain any ministry against his consent.   That no human authority can, in any case whatever, interfere with the rights of conscience; and that no preference shall ever be given to any religious establishment or mode of worship.

Sec. 4.   That the civil rights, privileges or capacities of any citizen shall in no wise be diminished or enlarged on account of his religion.

ARTICLE VII.

Sec. 2.   No person who denies the being of a God, shall hold any office in the civil department of this State, nor be allowed his oath in any court.

XXVI.   MICHIGAN, 1837.

75. Constitution of 1835.
Poore, 983.

ARTICLE I.

Sec. 4.   Every person has a right to worship Almighty God according to the dictates of his own conscience; and no person can of right be compelled to attend, erect, or support, against his will, any place of religious worship, or pay any tithes, taxes, or other rates for the support of any minister of the gospel or teacher of religion.

Sec. 5.   No money shall be drawn from the treasury for the benefit of religious societies, or theological or religious seminaries.

Sec. 6.   The civil and political rights, privileges, and capacities of no individual shall be diminished or enlarged on account of his opinions or belief concerning matters of religion.

D

Religious References in State Constitutions, A. D. 1837-1876.

XI. PENNSYLVANIA

76. Constitution of 1838.
Poore, 1564.
> Article IX, 3 and 4 same as in Constitution of 1790.

77. Constitution of 1873.
Poore, 1575.

From the Preamble

. . . grateful to the Almighty God for the blessings of civil and religious liberty, and humbly invoking his guidance, . . .

> ARTICLE I, Sec. 3 and 4 same as IX, 3 and 4, 1790.

ARTICLE III.

Sec. 17. No appropriation shall be made to any charitable or educational institution not under the absolute control of the Commonwealth, other than normal schools established by law for the professional training of teachers for the public schools of the state, except by a vote of two-thirds of all the members elected to each house.

Sec. 18. No appropriations, except for pensions or gratuities for military services shall be made for charitable, educational or benevolent purposes, to any person or community, nor to any denominational or sectarian institution, corporation or association.

ARTICLE IX.

Sec. 1.   . . . but the General Assembly may, by general laws, exempt from taxation public property used for public purposes, actual places of religious worship . . .

ARTICLE X

Sec. 2. No money raised for the support of public schools of the Commonwealth shall be appropriated to or used for the support of any sectarian school.

ARTICLE XI.

Sec. 1.   The General Assembly . . . may exempt from military service persons having conscientious scruples against bearing arms.

V.   RHODE ISLAND

78.   Constitution of Rhode Island, 1842.

Poore, 1603.

Preamble: . . . grateful to Almighty God for the civil and religious liberty which He hath so long permitted us to enjoy, and looking to Him for a blessing upon our endeavors . . .

ARTICLE I.

Sec. 3.   Whereas, Almighty God hath created the mind free; and all attempts to influence it by temporal punishments and burdens, or by civil incapacitations, tend to beget habits of hypocrisy and meanness; and whereas a principal object of our venerable ancestors, in their migration to this country and their settlement in this state, was, as they expressed it, to hold forth a lively experiment, that a flourishing civil state may stand and be best maintained with full liberty in religious concernments; we, therefore, declare that no man shall be compelled to frequent or to support any religious worship, place or ministry whatever, except in fulfillment of his own voluntary contract; nor enforced, restrained, molested, or burdened in his body or goods; nor disqualified from holding any office; or otherwise suffer on account of his religious belief; and that every man shall be free to worship God according to the dictates of his own conscience, and to profess and by argument to maintain his opinions in matters of religion; and that the same shall in no wise diminish, enlarge, or affect his civil capacity.

ARTICLE IX

Sec. 3.   . . . "So help me God."   Or, "This affirmation you make and give upon the peril of penalty of perjury.

VIII.   NEW JERSEY

79.   Constitution of 1844.

Poore, 1314.

Preamble: . . . grateful to Almighty God for the civil and religious liberty which He hath so long permitted us to enjoy, and looking to Him for a blessing upon our endeavors. . . .

ARTICLE I

Sec. 3. No person shall be deprived of the inestimable privilege of worshipping Almighty God in a manner agreeable to the dictates of his own conscience; nor, under any pretense whatever, to be compelled to attend any place of worship contrary to his faith and judgment; nor shall any person be obliged to pay tithes, taxes or other rates for building or repairing any church or churches, place or places of worship, or for the maintenance of any minister or ministry, contrary to what he believes to be right, or has deliberately and voluntarily engaged to perform.

Sec. 4. There shall be no establishment of one religious sect in preference to another; no religious test shall be required as a qualification for any office or public trust; and no person shall be denied the enjoyment of any civil right merely on account of his religious principles.

XXVII. FLORIDA, 1845.

80. Constitution of 1838.

Poore, 317.

ARTICLE I.

Sec. 3. That all men have a natural and inalienable right to worship Almighty God according to the dictates of their own conscience; and that no preference shall ever be given by law to any religious establishment or mode of worship in this State.

ARTICLE XIII

Sec. 1. The general assembly shall pass a general law for the incorporation of all such churches, and religious or other societies, as may accept thereof, but no special act of incorporation thereof shall be passed.

XXVIII. TEXAS, 1845.

81. Constitution of the Republic of Texas, 1836.

Poore, 1757.

ARTICLE V.

Section 1.   Ministers of the gospel being, by their profession, dedicated to God and care of souls, ought not to be diverted from the great duties of their functions; Therefore, no minister of the gospel, or priest of any denomination whatever, shall be eligible to the office of the executive of the republic, nor to a seat in either branch of the congress of the same.

DECLARATION OF RIGHTS

3d.   No preference shall be given by law to any religious denomination or mode of worship over another, but every person shall be permitted to worship God according to the dictates of his own conscience.

82.   Constitution of 1845.

Poore, 1767.

ARTICLE I

Sec. 3.   No religious test shall ever be required as a qualification to any office or public trust in this state.

Sec. 4.   All men have a natural and indefeasible right to worship Almighty God according to the dictates of their own consciences.   No man shall be compelled to attend, erect or support any place or worship, or maintain any ministry against his consent.   No human authority ought, in any case whatever, to control or interfere with the rights of conscience in matters of religion, and no preference shall ever be given by law to any religious society or mode of worship.   But it shall be the duty of the legislature to pass such laws as may be necessary to protect every religious denomination in the peaceable enjoyment of its own mode of public worship.

ARTICLE VI.

Sec. 2.   Any person who conscientiously scruples to bear arms shall not be compelled to do so, but shall pay an equivalent for personal service.

Sec. 3.   No licensed minister of the gospel shall be required to perform military duty, work on roads, or serve on juries in this state.

83.   Constitutions of 1866 and 1868.
      Religious sections in Art. I not altered.
      Article VI, 2 and 3 disappear 1868.
Poore 1784, 1801.

84.   Constitution of 1876.
Poore, 1824.

Preamble

Humbly invoking the blessing of Almighty God . . .

ARTICLE I

Sec. 4.   No religious test shall ever be required as a qualification to any office, or public trust, in this State; nor shall anyone be excluded from holding office on account of his religious sentiments, provided he acknowledges the existence of a Supreme Being.

Sec. 5.   No person shall be disqualified to give evidence in any of the courts of this State on account of his religious opinions, or for the want of any religious belief, but all oaths or affirmations shall be administered in the mode most binding upon the conscience, and shall be taken subject to the pains and penalties of perjury.

Sec. 6.   All men have a natural and indefeasible right to worship Almighty God according to the dictates of their own consciences.   No man shall be compelled to attend, erect, or support any place of worship, or to maintain any ministry against his consent.   No human authority ought in any case whatever, to control or interfere with the rights of conscience in matters of religion, and no preference shall be given by law to any religious society or mode of worship.   But it shall be the duty of the Legislature to pass such laws as may be necessary to protect equally every religious denomination in the peaceable enjoyment of its own mode of public worship.

Sec. 7.   No money shall be appropriated or drawn from the treasury for the benefit of any sect, or religious society, theological or religious seminary, nor shall property belonging to the State be appropriated for any such purpose.

ARTICLE VII.

Sec. 5.   . . . nor shall the same [permanent or available school fund] or any part thereof ever be appropriated to or used for the support of any sectarian school; . . .

ARTICLE VIII.

Sec. 2.   . . . but the legislature may, by general laws exempt from taxation . . . actual places of religious worship; [. . . also the endowment funds of such institutions of learning and religion not used with view to profit . . .]

ARTICLE XVI

Sec. 1.   . . . So help me God . . .

XXIX.   IOWA, 1846.

85.   Constitution of 1846.
Poore, 536.

From the Preamble

. . . grateful to the Supreme Being for the blessings hitherto enjoyed, and feeling our dependence on Him for the continuation of these blessings, . . .

ARTICLE I.

Sec. 3.   The General Assembly shall make no law respecting an establishment or religion, or prohibiting the free exercise thereof; nor shall any person be compelled to attend any place or worship, pay tithes, taxes, or other rates, for building or repairing places of worship, or the maintenance of any minister or ministry.

Sec. 4.   No religious test shall be required as a qualification for any office of public trust, and no person shall be deprived of any of his rights, privileges, capacities, or disqualified from the performance of any of his public or private duties, or rendered incompetent to give evidence in any court of law or equity, in consequence of his opinions on the subject of religion; and any party to any judicial proceeding shall have the right to use as a witness, or take the testimony of, any other person, not disqualified on account of interest, who may be cognizant of any fact material to the case; and parties to suits may be witnesses, as provided by Law.

ARTICLE VI.

Sec. 2. No person or persons conscientiously scrupulous of bearing arms shall be compelled to do military duty in time of peace; provided that such person or persons shall pay an equivalent, for such exemption in the same manner as other citizens.

ARTICLE VIII

Sec. 1. No corporation shall be created by special law; but the general assembly shall provide by general laws, for the organization of all corporations hereafter to be created, except as hereinafter provided.

86. Constitution of 1857.

Poore, 552.—no alterations in religious sections.

IX. NEW YORK

87. Constitution of 1846.

Poore, 1351.

Preamble

. . . grateful to Almighty God for our Freedom.

ARTICLE I.

Sec. 3. The free exercise and enjoyment of religious profession and worship, without discrimination or preference, shall forever be allowed in this state to all mankind; and no person shall be rendered incompetent to be a witness on account of his opinions on matters of religious belief; but the liberty of conscience hereby secured shall not be so construed as to excuse acts of licentiousness, or justify practices inconsistent with the peace and safety of this State.

ARTICLE XI

Section 1. The militia of this State shall, at all times hereafter, be armed and disciplined, and in readiness for service;

but all such inhabitants of this State, of any religious denomination whatever, as from scruples of conscience may be averse to bearing arms, shall be excused therefrom, upon such conditions as shall be prescribed by law.

XXX. WISCONSIN, 1848.

88. Constitution of 1848.
Poore, 2028.

From the Preamble

. . . grateful to Almighty God for our Freedom . . .

ARTICLE I

Sec. 18. The right of every man to worship Almighty God, according to the dictates of his own conscience, shall never be infringed; nor shall any man be compelled to attend, erect, or support any place of worship, or to maintain any ministry against his consent; nor shall any control of, or interference with, the rights of conscience be permitted, or any preference be given by law to any religious establishments, or modes of worship; nor shall any money be drawn from the treasury for the benefit of religious societies, or religious, or theological seminaries.

Sec. 19. No religious tests shall ever be required as a qualification for any office of public trust under the State, and no person shall be rendered incompetent to give evidence in any court of law, or equity, in consequence of his opinions on the subject of religion.

ARTICLE X

Sec. 3. The Legislature shall provide by law for the establishment of District Schools, which shall be as nearly uniform as practicable; and such schools shall be free and without charge for tuition, to all children between the ages of four and twenty years; and no sectarian instruction shall be allowed therein.

Sec. 6. (University Fund)
. . . and no sectarian instruction shall be allowed in such university.

ARTICLE XI

Sec. 1.   Corporations without banking powers or privileges may be formed under general laws.

XXI.   ILLINOIS

89.   Constitution of 1848.
Poore, 449.

From the Preamble

. . . grateful to Almighty God for the civil, political and religious liberty . . . and looking to Him for a blessing upon our endeavors.

ARTICLE VIII

Sec. 2.   Same as V, 2 of Constitution of 1818.

ARTICLE XIII

Sec. 3 and 4, same as VIII, 3, 4 of Constitution of 1818.

90.   Constitution of 1870.
Poore, 470.

Preamble as in 1848.

ARTICLE II.

Sec. 3.   The free exercise and enjoyment of religious profession and worship, without discrimination, shall forever be guaranteed; and no person shall be denied any civil or political right, privilege or capacity on account of his religious opinions; but the liberty of conscience hereby secured shall not be licentiousness, or justify practices inconsistent with the peace or safety of the State.   No person shall be required to attend or support any ministry or place of worship against his consent, nor shall any preference be given by law to any religious denomination or mode of worship.

Sec. 4.   Every person may freely speak, write, and publish on all subjects, being responsible for the abuse of that liberty . . .

ARTICLE IV.

Sec. 22. The General Assembly shall not pass local or special laws in any of the following enumerated cases, that is to say: for- . . . Granting to any corporation, association, or individual any special or exclusive privilege or immunity or franchise whatever.

ARTICLE VIII.

Sec. 3. Neither the general assembly nor any county, city, township, school-district or other public corporation shall ever make any appropriation, or pay from any public fund whatever, anything in aid of any church or sectarian purpose, or to help support or sustain any school, academy, seminary, college, university, or other literary or scientific institution, controlled by any church or sectarian denomination whatever; nor shall any grant or donation of land, money, or other personal property ever be made by the State or any such public corporation to any church or for any sectarian purpose.

ARTICLE IX

Sec. 3. The property of the State, counties, and other municipal corporations, both real and personal, and such other property as may be used exclusively for agricultural and horticultural societies, for school, religious, cemetery and charitable purposes, may be exempted from taxation . . .

ARTICLE XII.

Sec. 6. No person having conscientious scruples against bearing arms shall be compelled to do militia duty in time of peace . . .

XXXI. CALIFORNIA, 1850

91. Constitution of 1849.
Poore, 195.
Preamble
We, the people of the State of California, grateful to Almighty God for our freedom, in order to secure and perpetuate its blessings, do establish this constitution.

ARTICLE I.

Sec. 4.   The free exercise and enjoyment of religious profession and worship, without discrimination or preference, shall forever be guaranteed to this State; and no person shall be rendered incompetent to be a witness or juror on account of his opinions on matters of religious belief; but the liberty of conscience hereby secured shall not be construed as to excuse acts of licentiousness, or justify practices inconsistent with the peace or safety of this State.

XXVI.   MICHIGAN

92.   Constitution of 1850.

Poore, 999.

ARTICLE IV

Sec. 24.   The legislature may authorize the employment of a chaplain for the State prison; but no money shall be appropriated for the payment of any religious services in either house of the legislature.

Sec. 39.   The legislature shall pass no law to prevent any person from worshipping Almighty God according to the dictates of his own conscience, or to compel any person to attend, erect, or support any place of religious worship, or to pay tithes, taxes, or other rates for the support of any minister of the gospel or teacher of religion.

Sec. 40.   No money shall be appropriated or drawn from the treasury for the benefit of any religious sect or society, theological or religious seminary, nor shall property belonging to the State be appropriated for any such purposes.

Sec. 41.   The legislature shall not diminish or enlarge the civil or political rights, privileges, and capacities of any person on account of his opinion or belief concerning matters of religion.

ARTICLE VI.

Sec. 34.   No person shall be rendered incompetent to be a witness on account of his opinions on matters of religious belief.

ARTICLE XVIII

Sec. 1.   Oath of office does not contain: so help me God.

XV.   KENTUCKY

93.   Constitution of 1850, no changes in religious sections.
Poore, 684.

I.   VIRGINIA.

94.   Constitution of 1850.
Poore, 1921.

Article XVI of the Bill of Rights as in 1776.

ARTICLE IV.

Sec. 15.   The privilege of the writ of *habeas corpus* shall not in any case be suspended.   The general assembly shall not pass any bill of attainder; or any *ex post facto law;* or any law impairing the obligation of contracts; or any law whereby private property shall be taken for public uses without just compensation; or any law abridging the freedom of speech or of the press.   No man shall be compelled to frequent or support any religious worship, place, or ministry whatsoever; nor shall any man be enforced, restrained, molested, or burdened in his body or goods, or otherwise suffer, on account of his religious opinions in matters of religion, and the same shall in no wise affect, diminish, or enlarge their civil capacities.   And the general assembly shall not prescribe any religious test whatever; or confer any peculiar privileges or advantages on any sect or denomination; or pass any law requiring or authorizing any religious society, or the people of any district within this commonwealth, to levy on themselves or others any tax for the erection or repair of any house for public worship, or for the support of any church or ministry; but it shall be left free to every person to select his religious instructor, and to make for his support such private contract as he shall please.

Sec. 32.   The general assembly shall not grant a charter of incorporation to any church or religious denomination, but may secure the title to church property to an extent to be limited by law.

95.   Constitution of Virginia, 1870.
Poore, 1971.

Only changes affecting religion in Art. XI, sec. 7.

CHURCH PROPERTY

The rights of ecclesiastical bodies in and to church property conveyed to them by regular deed of conveyance shall not be affected by the late civil war, nor by any antecedent or subsequent event, nor by any act of the legislature purporting to govern the same, but all such property shall pass to and be held by the parties set forth in the original deeds of conveyance, or the legal assignees of such original parties holding through or by conveyance, and any act or acts of the legislature in opposition thereto shall be null and void.

XIX.   INDIANA

96.   Constitution of 1851.
Poore, 512.

From the Preamble

. . . grateful to Almighty God. . .

ARTICLE I.

Sec. 2.   All men shall be secured in their natural right to worship Almighty God according to the dictates of their own consciences.

Sec. 3.   No law shall, in any case, whatever, control the free exercise and enjoyment of religious opinions, or interfere with the rights of conscience.

Sec. 4.   No preference shall be given, by law, to any creed, religious society or mode of worship; and no man shall be made to attend, erect or support any place of worship, or maintain any ministry against his consent.

Sec. 5.   No religious test shall be required as a qualification for any office of trust or profit.

Sec. 6.   No money shall be drawn from the treasury for the benefit of any religious or theological institution.

Sec. 7. No person shall be rendered incompetent to witness, in consequence of his opinions on matters of religion.

Sec. 8. The mode of administering an oath or affirmation shall be such as may be most consistent with and binding upon the conscience of the person.

ARTICLE X.

Sec. 1. ... excepting such only for municipal, educational, literary, scientific, religious or charitable purposes, as may be specially exempt by law.

III. MARYLAND

97. Constitution of 1851.

Poore, 837.

... grateful to Almighty God...

ARTICLE 33 OF THE DECLARATION OF RIGHTS

That as it is the duty of every man to worship God in such manner as he thinks most acceptable to Him, all persons are equally entitled to protection in their religious liberty, wherefore, no person ought, by any law, to be molested in his person or estate on account of his religious persuasion or profession, or for his religious practice, unless under the color of religion any man shall disturb the good order, peace, or safety of the State, or shall infringe the laws of morality, or injure others in their natural, civil, or religious rights, nor ought any person to be compelled to frequent or maintain or contribute, unless on contract, to maintain any place of worship or any ministry; nor shall any person be deemed incompetent as a witness or juror who believes in the existence of a God, and that under his dispensation such person will be held morally accountable for his acts, and be rewarded or punished therefore, either in this world or the world to come.

ARTICLE 34 OF THE DECLARATION OF RIGHTS

That no other test or qualification ought to be required, on admission to any office of trust or profit, than such oath of office as may be prescribed by this constitution, or by the law of the State, and a declaration of belief in the Christian religion; and if the party shall profess to be a Jew, the declaration shall be of his belief in a future state of rewards and punishments.

ARTICLE 35 OF THE DECLARATION OF RIGHTS

That every gift, sale, or devise of land, to any minister, public teacher or preacher of the gospel, as such, or any religious sect, order, or denomination, . . . and every gift or sale of goods or chattels to go in succession, or to take place after the death of the seller or donor, to or for such support, use, or benefit; and also every devise of goods or chattels, to or for the support, use, or benefit of any minister, public teacher or preacher of the gospel, as such, or any religious sect, order or denomination, without the leave of the legislature, shall be void; except always any sale, gift, lease, or devise of any quantity of land, not exceeding five acres, for a church, meetinghouse, or other house of worship or parsonage, or for a burying-ground, which shall be improved, enjoyed, or used only for such purpose; or such sale, gift, lease, or devise shall be void.

ARTICLE 36 OF THE DECLARATION OF RIGHTS

That the manner of administering an oath or affirmation to any person ought to be such as those of the religious persuasion, profession or denomination of which he is a member generally esteem the most effectual confirmation by the attestation of the Divine Being.

98. Constitution of 1864.
Poore, 867.

ARTICLE 36 OF THE DECLARATION OF RIGHTS

Corresponds to Article 33 of Constitution of 1851.

ARTICLE 37 OF THE DECLARATION OF RIGHTS

That no other test or qualification ought to be required on admission to any office of trust or profit than such oath of allegiance and fidelity to this State and the United States as may be prescribed by this constitution, and such oath of office, and qualification as may be prescribed by this constitution, or by the laws of the State, and a declaration of belief in the Christian religion, or in the existence of God, and in a future state of rewards and punishments.

ARTICLE 38 OF THE DECLARATION OF RIGHTS

That every gift, sale or devise of land, to any minister, public teacher, or preacher of the gospel, as such, or to any religious sect, order or denomination, or to or for the support, use or benefit of, or in trust for any minister, public teacher, or preacher of the gospel, as such, or any religious sect, order or denomination; and every gift or sale of goods or chattels to go in succession, or to take place after the death of the seller or donor, to or for such support, use, or benefit of any minister, public teacher, or preacher of the gospel, as such; or any religious sect, order, or denomination, without the prior or subsequent sanction of the legislature, shall be void, except always any sale, gift, lease, or devise of any quantity of land, not exceeding five acres, for a church, meeting-house or other house of worship, or parsonage, or for a burying-ground, which shall be improved, enjoyed, or used only for such purpose, or such sale, gift lease, or devise shall be void.

ARTICLE 39 OF THE DECLARATION OF RIGHTS

Corresponds to Article 36 of Constitution of 1851.

99.   Constitution of 1867.
Poore, 888.

ARTICLE 36 OF THE DECLARATION OF RIGHTS

That as it is the duty of every man to worship God in such manner as he thinks most acceptable to Him, all persons are equally entitled to protection in their religious liberty; wherefore no person ought, by any law, to be molested in his person or estate on account of his religious persuasion or profession or for his religious practice, unless, under the color of religion he shall disturb the good order, peace or safety of the State, or shall infringe the laws of morality, or injure others in their natural civil or religious rights, nor ought any person to be compelled to frequent or maintain or contribute, unless on contract, to maintain any place of worship, or any ministry; nor shall any person, otherwise competent, be deemed incompetent as a witness, or juror, on account of his religious belief. Provided, he believes in the existence of God, and that, under his dispensation, such person will be held morally accountable for his acts, and be rewarded or punished therefore, either in this world or the world to come.

XVII. OHIO

100. Constitution of 1851.

Poore, 1466.

From the Preamble

. . . grateful to Almighty God for our freedom . . .

ARTICLE I.

Sec. 7. All men have a natural and indefeasible right to worship Almighty God according to the dictates of their own conscience. No person shall be compelled to attend, erect, or maintain any form of worship, against his consent and no preference shall be given, by law, to any religious society; nor shall any intereference with the rights of conscience be permitted. No religious test shall be required, as a qualification for office, nor shall any person be incompetent to be a witness on account of his religious belief; but nothing herein shall be construed to dispense with oaths and affirmations. Religion, morality and knowledge, however, being essential to good government, it shall be the duty of the general assembly to pass suitable laws to protect every religious denomination in the peaceable enjoyment of its own mode of public worship, and to encourage schools, and the means of instruction.

ARTICLE VI.

Sec. 1. The principal of all funds, arising from the sale, or other disposition of lands, or other property, granted or entrusted to this state for educational and religious purposes, shall forever be preserved inviolate.

Sec. 2. The general assembly shall make such provisions,

by taxation, or otherwise, as, with the income arising from the school trust fund, will secure a thorough and efficient system of common schools throughout the state; but no religious or other sect, or sects, shall ever have any exclusive right to, or control of, any part of the school funds of this state.

ARTICLE XII.

Sec. 2. . . . but burying grounds, public school houses, houses used exclusively for public worship, institutions used exclusively for charitable purposes, public property used exclusively for public purposes, . . . may, by general laws, be exempt from taxation. . . .

XXXII.   MINNESOTA, 1858.

101.   Constitution of 1857.
Poore, 1029.

From Preamble

. . . grateful to God for our civil and religious liberty . . .

ARTICLE I.

Sec. 16.   The enumeration of rights in this constitution shall not be construed to deny or impair others retained by and inherent in the people.   The right of every man to worship God according to the dictates of his own conscience shall never be infringed, nor shall any man be compelled to attend, erect or support any place of worship, or to maintain any religious or ecclesiastical ministry, against his consent; nor shall any control of or interference with the rights of conscience be permitted, or any preference be given by law to any religious establishment or mode of worship; but the liberty of conscience hereby secured shall not be construed as to excuse acts of licentiousness, or to justify practices inconsistent with the peace and safety of the State, nor shall any money be drawn from the treasury for the benefit of any religious societies, or religious or theological seminaries.

Sec. 17.   No religious test or amount of property shall ever be required as a qualification for any office of public trust under this State.   No religous test or amount of property shall

ever be required as a qualification of any voter at any election
in this State; nor shall any person be rendered incompetent to
give evidence in any court of law or equity in consequence of
his opinion upon the subject of religion.

ARTICLE IX.

Sec. 3. . . . but public burying grounds, public school
houses, public hospitals, academies, colleges, universities, and
all seminaries, colleges, universities, and all seminaries of learning, all churches, church property, and houses of worship, institutions of purely public charity, and public property used exclusively for public purposes, shall be exempt from taxation.

XXXIII.   OREGON, 1859.

102.   Constitution of 1857.
Poore, 1492.

ARTICLE I.

Sec. 2.   All men shall be secured in their natural right to
worship Almighty God according to the dictates of their own
consciences.

Sec. 3.   No law shall, in any case whatever, control the
free exercise and enjoyment of religious opinions, or interfere
with the rights of conscience.

Sec. 4.   No religious test shall be required as a qualification for any office of trust or profit.

Sec. 5.   No money shall be drawn from the treasury for
the benefit of any religious or theological institution nor shall
any money be appropriated for the payment of any religious
service in either house of the Legislative Assembly.

Sec. 6.   No person shall be rendered incompetent as a witness or juror in consequence of his opinions on matters of religion, nor be questioned in any court of justice touching his
religious belief, to affect the weight of his testimony.

Sec. 8.   No law shall be passed restraining the free ex-
pression of opinion, nor restricting the right to speak, write, or
print freely on any subject whatever; but every person shall be
responsible for the abuse of this right.

ARTICLE IX.

Sec. 1. The legislative assembly shall provide by law for uniform and equal rate of assessment and taxation and shall prescribe regulations and shall secure a just valuation for taxation of all property, both real and personal, excepting such only for municipal, educational, literary, scientific, religious, or charitable purposes as may be specially exempted by law.

ARTICLE X.

Sec. 2. (Militia) Persons whose religious tenets or conscientious scruples forbid them to bear arms, shall not be compelled to do so in time of peace; but shall pay an equivalent for such personal service.

XXXIV. KANSAS, 1861.

103.   Constitution of 1855.
Poore, 581.

ARTICLE I.

Sec. 7. All men have a natural and indefeasible right to worship Almighty God according to the dictates of their own conscience. No person shall be compelled to attend, erect, or support any place of worship, or maintain any form of worship against his consent; and no preference shall be given by law to any religious society, nor shall any interference with the rights of conscience be permitted. No religious test shall be required as a qualification for office, nor shall any person be incompetent to be a witness on account of his religious belief; but nothing herein shall be construed to dispense with oaths and affirmations. Religion, morality, and knowledge, however, being essential to good government, it shall be the duty of the general assembly to pass suitable laws to protect every religious denomination in the peaceable enjoyment of its own mode of public worship, and to encourage schools and the means of instruction.

ARTICLE X

Sec. 6. No person conscientiously opposed to bearing arms shall be compelled to do militia duty, but such person shall pay an equivalent for such exemption, the amount to be prescribed by law.

ARTICLE XI.

Sec. 1.   The general assembly shall provide by law for a uniform and equal rate of assessment and taxation, and taxes shall be levied upon all such property, real and personal, as the general assembly may from time to time prescribe; but all property appropriated and used exclusively for municipal, literary, educational, scientific, or charitable purposes, and personal property to an amount not exceeding one hundred dollars for each head of a family, and all property appropriated and used exclusively for religious purposes, to an amount not exceeding two hundred thousand dollares, may by general laws be exempted from taxation.

104.   Constitution of 1857,
Poore, 599.

ARTICLE XIII.

Sec. 2.   Any citizen whose religious tenets conflict with bearing arms, shall not be compelled to do militia duty in time of peace, but shall pay such an equivalent for personal services as may be prescribed by law.

Bill of Rights.

3.   That all persons have a natural and indefeasible right to worship Almighty God according to the dictates of their own conscience, and no person can of right be compelled to attend, erect, or support any place of worship or maintain any ministry against his consent.   That no human authority can in any case whatever interfere with the rights of conscience, and that no preference shall ever be given to any religious establishment or mode of worship.

4.   That the civil rights, privileges, or capacities of a citizen shall in nowise be diminished or enlarged on account of his religion.

105.   Constitution of 1858.
Poore, 614.

ARTICLE I

Sec. 7.   corresponds to I, Sec. 7 of 1855.

ARTICLE XIV.

Sec. 3.   The property of corporations, except for charitable and religious purposes, now existing and to be hereafter created, shall be subject to taxation the same as the property of individuals.

Sec. 4.   All real estate or other property of religious corporations shall vest in trustees, whose election shall be by the members of such corporation.

106.   Constitution of 1859.

Poore, 630.

From the Preamble

. . . grateful to Almighty God for our civil and religious privileges. . .

Bill of Rights

Sec. 7.   The right to worship God according to the dictates of conscience shall never be infringed, nor shall any person be compelled to attend or support any form of worship; nor shall any control of or interference with the rights of conscience be permitted, nor any preference be given by law to any religious establishment or mode of worship.   No religious test or property qualification shall be required for any office of public trust, nor for any vote at any election; nor shall any person be incompetent to testify on account of religious belief.

ARTICLE VI.

Sec. 8.   No religious sect or sects shall ever control any part of the common-school or university funds of the state.

ARTICLE VIII.

Sec. 1.   . . . but all citizens, of any religious denomination whatever, who, from scruples of conscience, may be averse to bearing arms shall be exempted therefrom, upon such conditions as may be prescribed by law.

ARTICLE XI.

Sec. 1.   The legislature shall provide for a uniform and equal rate of assessment and taxation: but all property used exclusively for state, county, municipal, literary, educational, scientific, religious, benevolent and charitable purposes, and personal property to the amount of at least two hundred dollars for each family, shall be exempted from taxation.

ARTICLE XII.

Sec. 1. (Corporations) . . . Corporations may be created under general laws. . .

Sec. 3. The title to all property of religious corporations shall vest in trustees, whose election shall be by the members of such corporations.

XXXV. WEST VIRGINIA, 1863.

107. Constitution of 1861-63,
Poore, 1978.

ARTICLE II.

Sec. 9. No man shall be compelled to frequent or support any religious worship, place or ministry whatsoever; nor shall any man be enforced, restrained, molested or burdened, in his body or goods, or otherwise suffer, on account of his religious opinions or belief, but all men shall be free to profess, and by argument, to maintain their opinions in matters of religion and the same shall, in no wise, affect, diminish or enlarge their civil capacities; and the legislature shall not prescribe any religious test what ever, or confer any peculiar privileges or advantages on any sect or denomination, or pass any law requiring or authorizing any religious society, or people of any district within this State, to levy on themselves, or others, any tax for the erection or repair of any house for public worship, or for the support of any church or ministry, but it shall be left free for every person to select his religious instructor, and to make for his support, such private contract as he shall please.

ARTICLE VIII.

Sec. 1. . . . property used for . . . religious and charitable purposes, . . . may, by law, be exempted from taxation.

ARTICLE XI.

Sec. 2.   No charter of incorporation shall be granted to any church or religious denomination.   Provision may be made by general laws for securing the title to church property, so that it shall be held and used for the purpose intended.
108.   Constitution of 1872.

Poore, 1993.

ARTICLE III.

Sec. 11.   . . . No religious or political test oath shall be required as a prerequisite or qualification to vote, serve as a juror, sue, plead, appeal, or pursue any profession or employment;

Sec. 15 corresponds to II, sec. 9 of Constitution of 1861.

ARTICLE VI.

Sec. 30.   The Legislature shall not pass local or special laws in any of the following enumerated cases; that is to say for . . .
Providing for the sale of church property, or property held for charitable uses.

Sec. 47.   No charter of incorporation shall be granted to any church or religious denomination.   Provision shall be made by general laws for securing the titles to church property, and for the sale and transfer thereof, so that it shall be held, used, or transferred for the purpose of such church or religious denomination.

ARTICLE X.

Sec. 1.   . . . but property used for educational, literary, scientific, religious or charitable purposes . . . may be exempted from taxation.

XXXVI.   NEVADA, 1864.

109.   Enabling Act for Nevada, 1864.
Poore, 1246.

Sec. 4.   Second, that perfect toleration of religious sentiment shall be secured, and no inhabitant of said state shall ever be molested, in person or property, on account of his or her mode of religious worship.

110.   Constitution of 1864.

From Preamble.

. . . grateful to Almighty God for our freedom . . .

ARTICLE I.

Sec. 4.   The free exercise and enjoyment of religious profession and worship without discrimination or preference, shall forever be allowed in this state; and no person shall be rendered incompetent to be a witness on account of his opinions on matters of his religious belief; but the liberty of conscience hereby secured shall not be so construed as to excuse acts of licentiousness, or justify practices inconsistent with the peace or safety of this state.

ARTICLE VIII

Sec. 2.   All real property and possessory rights to the same, as well as personal property in this state, belonging to corporations now existing or hereafter created, shall be subject to taxation the same as property of individuals; provided, that the property of corporations formed for municipal, charitable, religious or educational purposes may be exempted by law.

ARTICLE XI.

Sec. 9.   No sectarian instruction shall be imparted or tolerated in any school or university that may be established under this constitution.

XXV.   ARKANSAS

111.   Constitution of 1864.
Poore, 121.

ARTICLE II.

Sec. 3.   Corresponds to II, 3 of Constitution of 1836.

Sec. 4.   That the civil rights, privileges or capacities of any citizen shall in no wise be diminished or enlarged on account of his religion.

ARTICLE VIII

Sec. 3. No person who denies the being of a God shall hold any office in the civil department of this State, nor be allowed his oath in any court.

112.   Constitution of 1868.

Poore, 134.

From Preamble.

. . . grateful to God for our civil and religious liberty . . .

ARTICLE I.

Sec. 21. No religious test or amount of property shall ever be required as a qualification for any office of public trust under the State. No religious test or amount of property shall ever be required as a qualification of any voter at any election in this State; nor shall any person be rendered incompetent to give evidence in any court of law or equity in consequence of his opinion upon the subject or religion; and the mode of administering an oath or affirmation shall be such as shall be most consistent with, and binding upon the conscience of the person to whom such oath or affirmation may be administered.

Sec. 23. Religion, morality and knowledge being essential to good government, the general assembly shall pass suitable laws to protect every religious denomination in the peaceable enjoyment of its own mode of public worship; and to encourage schools and the means of instruction.

113.   Constitution of 1874.

Poore, 154.

Preamble

We, the people of the State of Arkansas, grateful to Almighty God for the privilege of choosing our own form of government, for our civil and religious liberty, and desiring to perpetuate its blessings and secure the same to ourselves and posterity, do ordain and establish this constitution.

ARTICLE II.

Sec. 24. All men have a natural and indefeasible right to worship Almighty God according to the dictates of their own consciences; no man can, of right, be compelled to attend, erect or support any place of worship; or maintain any ministry against his consent. No human authority can, in any case or manner whatsoever, control or interfere with the right of conscience; and no preference shall ever be given, by law, to any religious establishment, denomination or mode of worship above any other.

Sec. 25. Religion, morality and knowledge being essential to good government, the general assembly shall enact suitable laws to protect every religious denomination in the peaceable enjoyment of its own mode of public worship.

Sec. 26. No religious test shall ever be required of any person as a qualification to vote or hold office, nor shall any person be rendered incompetent to be a witness on account of his religious belief; but nothing herein shall be construed to dispense with oaths or affirmations.

ARTICLE XIV.

Sec. 2. No money or property belonging to the public school fund, or to this State for the benefit of schools or universities, shall ever be used for any other than for the respective purposes to which it belongs.

ARTICLE XVI

Sec. 5. . . . that the following property shall be exempt from taxation . . . churches used as such.

ARTICLE XIX

Sec. 1. No person who denies the being of God shall hold any office in the civil departments of this State, nor be competent to testify as a witness in any court.

XVIII. LOUISIANA

114. Constitution of 1864.

Poore, 751.

Art. 124. . . . The general assembly shall have power to exempt from taxation property actually used for church, school, or charitable purposes.

Art. 146.   No appropriation shall be made by the legislature for the support of any private school or institution of learning whatever . . .

115.   Constitution of 1868.

Poore, 755.

Article 12.   Every person has the natural right to worship God according to the dictates of his conscience.   No religious test shall be required as a qualification for office.

Article 118.   . . . The general assembly shall levy a poll-tax on all male inhabitants of this State, over twenty-one years old, for school and charitable purposes, which tax shall never exceed one dollar and fifty cents per annum.

XXII.   ALABAMA

116.   Constitution of 1865.

Poore, 48.

ARTICLE I

Sec. 3.   That no person within this State shall, upon any pretence whatever, be deprived of the inestimable privilege of worshipping God in the manner most agreeable to his own conscience; nor be hurt, molested, or restrained in his religious profession, sentiments, or persuasions, provided he does not disturb others in their religious worship.

Sec. 4.   That no religion shall be established by law, that no preference shall be given by law to any religious sect, society denomination or mode of worship; that no one shall be compelled by law to attend any place of worship; nor to pay any tithes, taxes, or other rates for building or repairing any place of worship, or for maintaining any minister or ministry, that no religious test shall be required as a qualification to any office or public trust under this State; and that civil rights, privileges and capacities of any citizen shall not be in any manner affected by his religious principles.

117.   Constitution of 1867.

Poore, 60.

From Preamble

. . . invoking the favor and guidance of Almighty God . . .

ARTICLE I.

Sec. 4.   That no person shall be deprived of the right to worship God according to the dictates of his own conscience.

Sec. 5.   That no religion shall be established by law.

ARTICLE X.

Sec. 1.   . . . but all citizens of any denomination whatever, who, from scruples of conscience, may be averse to bearing arms, shall be exempt therefrom under such conditions as may be prescribed by law.

118.   Constitution of 1875.

Poore, 76.

From Preamble

. . . profoundly grateful to Almighty God for this inestimable right and invoking his favor and guidance . . .

ARTICLE I

Sec. 4 corresponds to I, 4, 1865.

XXIV.   MISSOURI.

119.   Constitution of 1865.

Poore, 1136.

From Preamble

. . . grateful to Almighty God, the sovereign ruler of the nations . . . and acknowledging our dependence upon Him for the continuance of those blessings . . .

ARTICLE I.

9.   That all men have a natural and indefeasible right to worship Almighty God according to the dictates of their own conscience; that no person can, on account of his religious opinions, be rendered ineligible to any office of trust or profit under this State, nor be disqualified from testifying, or from serving as a juror; that no human authority can control or interfere with the rights of conscience; that no person ought, by any law, to be molested in his person or estate, on account of his

religious persuasion or profession; but the liberty of conscience hereby secured shall not be so construed as to excuse acts of licentiousness, nor to justify practices inconsistent with good order, peace or safety of this State, or with the rights of others.

10.   That no person can be compelled to erect, support or attend any place or system of worship, or to maintain or support any priest, minister, preacher or teacher of any sect, church, creed or denomination of religion; but if any person shall voluntarily make a contract for any such object, he shall be held to the performance of the same.

11.   That no preference can ever be given by law to any church, sect, or mode of worship.

12.   That no religious corporation can be established in this State; except that by a general law, uniform throughout the State, any church, or religious society, or congregation, may become a body-corporate, for the sole purpose of acquiring, holding, using, and disposing of so much land as may be required for a house of public worship, a chapel, a parsonage, and a burial-ground, and managing the same, and contracting in relation to such land, and the buildings thereon, through a board of trustees, selected by themselves; but the quantity of land to be held by any such body-corporate, in connection with a house of worship or a parsonage, shall not exceed five acres in the country, or one acre in town or city.

13.   That every gift, sale, or devise of land to any minister, public teacher, or preacher of the gospel, as such, or to any religious sect, order, or denomination; or to or for the support, use, or benefit of, or in trust for, any minister, public teacher, or preacher of the gospel, as such, or any religious sect, order, or denomination; and every gift or sale of goods or chattels to go in succession, or to take place after the death of the seller or donor, to or for such support, use, or benefit; and also every devise of goods or chattels, to or for the support, use, or benefit of any minister, public teacher, or preacher of the gospel, as such, or any religious sect, order, or denomination, shall be void; except always any gift, sale, or devise of land to a church, religious society, or congregation, or to any person or persons in trust for the use of a church, religious society, or congregation, whether incorporated or not, for the uses and purposes, and within the limitations, of the next preceding clause of this article.

ARTICLE II.

Sec. 9.   No person shall assume the duties of any State, county, city, town, or other office, to which he may be appointed, otherwise than by a vote of the people; nor shall any person, after the expiration of sixty days after this constitution takes effect, be permitted to practise as an attorney or counsellor at law; nor, after that time, shall any person be competent as a bishop, priest, deacon, minister, elder or other clergyman of any religious persuasion, sect or denomination, to teach or preach, or solemnize marriages, unless such person shall have first taken, subscribed, and filed said oath.

120.   Constitution of 1875.

Poore, 1165.

From the Preamble.

. . . with profound reverence for the Supreme Ruler of the Universe, and grateful for His goodness. . . .

ARTICLE II.

Sec. 5 corresponds to I, 9 of Constitution of 1865.

Sec. 6.   That no person can be compelled to erect, support or attend any place or system of worship, or to maintain or support any priest, minister, preacher or teacher of any sect, church, creed or denomination of religion; but if any person shall voluntarily make a contract for any such object, he shall be held to the performance of the same.

Sec. 7.   That no money shall ever be taken from the public treasury, directly or indirectly, in aid of any church, sect or denomination of religion, or in aid of any priest, preacher, minister, or teacher thereof, as such; and that no preference shall be given to nor any discrimination made against any church, sect or creed of religion, or any form of religious faith or worship.

Sec. 8.   That no religious corporation can be established in this State, except such as may be created under a general law for the purpose only of holding title to such real estate as may be prescribed by law for church edifices, parsonages, and cemeteries.

ARTICLE IV

Sec. 53.   The general assembly shall not pass any local or special laws . . .

Exempting property from taxation.

Creating corporations, or amending, renewing, extending or explaining the charter thereof.

Granting to any corporation, association, or individual any special or exclusive right, privilege, or immunity, or to any corporation, association or individual the right to lay down a railroad track.

ARTICLE X

Sec. 6. The property, real and personal, of the state, counties and other municipal corporations, and cemeteries, shall be exempt from taxation. Lots in incorporated cities or towns, or within one mile of the limits of any such city or town, to the extent of one acre, and lots one mile or more distant from such cities or towns, to the extent of five acres, with the buildings thereon, may be exempted from taxation, when the same are used exclusively for religious worship, for schools, or for purposes purely charitable; also, such property, real or personal, as may be used exclusively for agricultural or horticultural societies: Provided, that such exemptions shall be only by general law.

ARTICLE XI

Sec. 11. Neither the general assembly nor any county, city, town, township, school district, or other municipal corporation, shall ever make an appropriation or pay from any public fund whatever, anything in aid of any religious creed, church or sectarian purpose, or to help support or sustain any private or public school, academy, seminary, college, university or other institution of learning, controlled by any religious creed, church or sectarian denomination whatever; nor shall any grant or donation of personal property or real estate ever be made by the state, or any county, city, town or other municipal corporation, for any religious creed, church, or sectarian purpose whatever.

ARTICLE XIII.

Sec. 1. . . . Provided, that no person who is religiously scrupulous of bearing arms can be compelled to do so, but may be compelled to pay an equivalent for military service in such manner as shall be prescribed by law.

XXXVII. NEBRASKA, 1867

121.   Constitution of 1866/67.

Poore, 1203.

From Preamble

. . . grateful to Almighty God for our freedom . . .

ARTICLE I.

Sec. 16.   All men have a natural and indefeasible right to worship Almighty God according to the dictates of their own conscience.   No person shall be compelled to attend, erect or support any place of worship against his consent, and no preference shall be given by law to any religious society, nor shall any interference of conscience be permitted.   No religious test shall be required as a qualification for office, nor shall any person be incompetent to witness on account of his religious belief; but nothing herein shall be construed to dispense with oaths or affirmations.   Religion, morality and knowledge, however, being essential to good government, it shall be the duty of the legislature to pass suitable laws to protect every religious denomination in the peaceable enjoyment of its own mode of worship, and to encourage schools and the means of instruction.

122.   Constitution of 1875.

Poore, 1214.

ARTICLE I.

Sec. 4.   Corresponds to I, 16 of Constitution of 1866/67.

ARTICLE III.

Sec. 15.   The legislature shall not pass local or special laws in any of the following cases, that is to say . . .

Granting to any corporation, association or individual any special or exclusive privileges, immunity, or franchise whatever . . .

ARTICLE VIII.

Sec. 11.   No sectarian instruction shall be allowed in any school or institution supported in whole or in part by the public funds set apart for educational purposes; nor shall the state accept any grant, conveyance, or bequest of money, lands or other property to be used for sectarian purposes.

ARTICLE IX.

Sec. 2. . . . for school, religious, cemetery, and charitable purposes, may be exempted from taxation, but such exemptions shall be by general law. . .

ARTICLE XII.

Sec. 3. The credit of the state shall never be given or loaned in aid of any individual, association, or corporation.

XIII. GEORGIA

123. Constitution of 1865.
Poore, 402.

From Preamble

. . . acknowledging and invoking the guidance of Almighty God, the author of all good government. . .

ARTICLE I.

Five. Perfect freedom of religious sentiment be, and the same is hereby, secured, and no inhabitant of this State shall ever be molested in person or property, nor prohibited from holding any public office or trust, on account of his religious opinions.

124. Constitution of 1868.
Poore, 411.

ARTICLE I.

Sec. 6. Perfect freedom of religious sentiment shall be, and the same is hereby, secured, and no inhabitant of this State shall ever be molested in person or property, or prohibited from holding any public office or trust, on account of his religious opinion; but the liberty of conscience hereby secured shall not be so construed as to excuse acts of licentiousness or justify practices inconsistent with the peace or safety of the people.

ARTICLE VIII.

Sec. 3. No person conscientiously opposed to bearing arms shall be compelled to do militia duty, but such person shall pay an equivalent for exemption; the amount to be prescribed by law and appropriated to the common-school fund.

125. Constitution of the United States.

AMENDMENT XIV, 1868

1. All persons born or naturalized in the United States, and subject to the jurisdiction thereof, are citizens of the United States and of the State wherein they reside. No State shall make or enforce any law which shall abridge the privileges or immunities of citizens of the United States; nor shall any State deprive any person of life, liberty, or property without due process of law, nor deny to any person within its jurisdiction the equal protection of the laws.

XX. MISSISSIPPI

126. Constitution of 1868.
Poore, 1081.
From the Preamble.

. . . grateful to Almighty God for the free exercise of the right to choose our own form of government.

ARTICLE I.

Sec. 21. No public money or moneys shall be appropriated for any charitable or other public institutions in this State making any distinction among the citizens thereof: *Provided,* That nothing herein contained shall be so construed as to prevent the legislature from appropriating the school-fund in accordance with the article in this constitution relating to public schools.

Sec. 23. No religious test as a qualification for office shall ever be required, and no preference shall ever be given by law to any religious sect or mode of worship, but the free enjoyment of all religious sentiments and the different modes of worship shall ever be held sacred: *Provided,* The rights hereby secured shall not be construed to justify acts of licentiousness injurious to morals or dangerous to the peace and safety of the State.

ARTICLE VIII.

Sec. 9.   No religious sect or sects shall ever control any part of the school or university funds of this state.

ARTICLE XII.

Sec. 3.   No person who denies the existence of a Supreme Being shall hold any office in this state.

Sec. 26.   Oath of office: So help me God.

VII.   SOUTH CAROLINA

127.   Constitution of 1865.

Poore, 1637.

Article I, Sec. 30, corresponds to XXI of 1778.

ARTICLE IX.

Sec. 8.   The free exercise and enjoyment of religious profession and worship, without discrimination or preference, shall be allowed within this State to all mankind: *Provided,* That the liberty of conscience hereby declared shall not be construed as to excuse acts of licentiousness, or justify practices inconsistent with the peace and safety of the State.

Sec. 9.   The rights, privileges, immunities, and estates of both civil and religious societies and of corporate bodies shall remain as if the constitution of this State had not been altered or amended.

128.   Constitution of 1868.

Poore, 1646.

Preamble

We, the people of the State of South Carolina, in convention assembled, grateful to Almighty God for this opportunity, deliberately and peaceably, of entering into an explicit and solemn compact with each other, and forming a new constitution of civil government for ourselves and posterity, recognizing the necessity of the protection of the people in all that pertains to their freedom, safety, and tranquillity, and imploring the direction of the Great Legislator of the universe, do agree upon, ordain, and establish the following declaration of rights and form of government as the constitution of the commonwealth of South Carolina:

ARTICLE I.

Sec. 9. No person shall be deprived of the right to worship God according to the dictates of his own conscience: *Provided,* That the liberty of conscience hereby declared shall not justify practices inconsistent with the peace and moral safety of society.

Sec. 10. No form of religion shall be established by law; but it shall be the duty of the general assembly to pass suitable laws to protect every religious denomination in the peaceable enjoyment of its own mode of worship.

ARTICLE XIV.

Sec. 6. No person who denies the existence of the Supreme Being shall hold any office under this constitution.

VI. NORTH CAROLINA

129. Constitution of 1868.
Poore, 1419.

From the Preamble

. . ., grateful to Almighty God, the Sovereign Ruler of Nations for the preservation of the American Union and the existence of our civil, political and religious liberties, and acknowledging our dependence upon Him for the continuance of those blessings to us. . . .

ARTICLE I.

Sec. 26. All men have a natural and unalienable right to worship Almighty God according to the dictates of their own consciences, and no human authority should, in any case whatever, control or interfere with the rights of conscience.

ARTICLE V.

Sec. 6.   ... The assembly may exempt cemeteries and property held for educational, scientific, literary, charitable or religious purposes ...

ARTICLE VI.

Sec. 4.   ... So help me God ...
Sec. 5.   The following classes of persons shall be disqualified for office: First, all persons who shall deny the being of Almighty God...

ARTICLE IX.

Sec. 1.   Religion, morality and knowledge being necessary to good government and the happiness of mankind, schools and the means of education shall forever be encouraged.
Sec. 4.   ... shall be faithfully appropriated for establishing and maintaining in this State a system of free public schools, and for no other uses or purposes whatsoever.

ARTICLE XII.

Sec. 1.   ... Provided, that all persons who may be averse to bearing arms, from religious scruples, shall be exempt therefrom.

130.   Constitution of 1876.
Poore, 1436.

Religious clauses of Constitution of 1868 continued.

XVI.   TENNESSEE.

131.   Constitution of 1870.
Poore, 1694.

ARTICLE I.

Sec. 3.   Corresponds to I, 3 of Constitution of 1834.

Sec. 4.   That no political or religious test, other than an oath to support the Constitution of the United States and of this State, shall ever be required as a qualification to any office or public trust under this State.

Sec. 6.   . . . No religious test for jurors.

Sec. 28.   That no citizen of this State shall be compelled to bear arms, provided he will pay an equivalent to be ascertained by law.

ARTICLE II.

Sec. 28.   All property, real, personal, or mixed, shall be taxed; but the legislature may exempt such as may be . . . used for purposes purely religious, . . .

Sec. 31.   The credit of this State shall not be hereafter loaned or given to or in aid of any person, association, corporation, municipality.

ARTICLE VIII.

Sec. 3.   The legislature shall pass laws exempting citizens belonging to any sect or denomination of religion, the tenets of which are known to be opposed to the bearing of arms, from attending private and general musters.

ARTICLE IX.

Sec. 1.   Whereas ministers of the gospel are, by their profession, dedicated to God, and the care of souls, and ought not to be diverted from the great duties of their functions; therefore no minister of the gospel, or priest of any denomination whatever, shall be eligible to a seat in either house of the Legislature.

Sec. 2.   No person who denies the being of God, or a future state of rewards and punishments, shall hold any office in the civil department of this state.

ARTICLE XI.

Sec. 8.   . . . No corporation shall be created, or its powers increased or diminished, by special laws; but the general assembly shall provide by general laws for the organization of all corporations hereafter created. . . .

Sec. 15.   No person shall, in time of peace, be required to perform any service to the public on any day set apart by his religion as a day of rest.

XXXVIII.   COLORADO, 1876.

132.   Constitution of 1876.

Poore, 219.

Preamble

We, the people of Colorado, with profound reverence for the Supreme Ruler of the Universe, in order to form a more independent and perfect government, establish justice, insure tranquility, provide for the common defence; promote the general welfare, and secure the blessings of liberty to ourselves and to our posterity, do ordain and establish this constitution for the State of Colorado.

ARTICLE II.

Sec. 4.   That the free exercise and the enjoyment of religious profession and worship, without discrimination, shall forever hereafter be guaranteed; and no person shall be denied any civil or political right, privilege, or capacity on account of his opinions concerning religion; but the liberty of conscience hereby secured shall not be construed to dispense with oaths or affirmations, excuse acts of licentiousness, or justify practices inconsistent with the good order, peace or safety of the State.   No person shall be required to attend or support any ministry or place of worship, religious sect or denomination against his consent; nor shall any preference be given by law to any religious denomination or mode of worship.

ARTICLE V.

Sec. 34.   No appropriation shall be made for charitable, industrial, educational, or benevolent purposes to any person, corporation, or community not under the absolute control of the State, nor to any denominational or sectarian institution or association.

ARTICLE IX.

Sec. 7.   Neither the general assembly, nor any county, city, town, township, school-district, or other public corporation shall ever make any appropriation, or pay from any public fund or moneys, whatever, anything in aid to any church or sectarian society, or for any sectarian purpose, or to help support or sustain any school, academy, seminary, college, university, or other literary or scientific institution controlled by any church or sectarian denomination whatsoever; nor shall any grant or donation of land, money, or other personal property ever be made by the State, or any other public corporation, to any church or for any sectarian purpose.

Sec. 8.   No religious test or qualification shall ever be required of any person as a condition of admission into any public educational institution of the State, either as teacher or student, and no teacher or student of any such institution shall ever be required to attend or participate in any religious service whatsoever.   No sectarian tenets or doctrines shall ever be taught in the public schools, nor shall any distinction or classification of pupils be made on account of race or color.

ARTICLE X.

Sec. 5.   Lots, with the buildings thereon, if said buildings are used solely and exclusively for religious worship, for schools, or for strictly charitable purposes, also cemeteries not used or held for private or corporate profit, shall be exempt from taxation, unless otherwise provided by the general law.

ARTICLE XVII.

Sec. 5.   No person having conscientious scruples against bearing arms shall be compelled to do militia duty in time of peace; provided, Such person shall pay an equivalent for such exemption.

E.

Religious References in State Constitutions, A. D. 1876 to 1930.

XIII. GEORGIA

133. Constitution of 1877.

Kettleborough, 310.

ARTICLE I, Sec. I.

Par. 12. All men have the natural and inalienable right to worship God, each according to the dictates of his own conscience, and no human authority should in any case control or interfere with such right of conscience.

Par. 13. No inhabitant of this State shall be molested in person or property, or prohibited from holding any public office or trust, on account of his religious opinions; but the right of liberty of conscience shall not be so construed as to excuse acts of licentiousness, or justify practises inconsistent with the peace and safety of the State.

Par. 14. No money shall ever be taken from the public treasury, directly or indirectly, in aid of any church, sect, or denomination of religionists, or of any sectarian institution.

ARTICLE VII.

Sec. 2. Par. 2. The General Assembly may, by law, exempt from taxation all public property; places of religious worship or burial; . . . or any seminary of learning.

XXXVI. NEVADA.

134. Article XI.   Sec. 10, 1880.

No public funds of any kind or character whatever, state, county, or municipal, shall be used for sectarian purposes.

XXVII. FLORIDA.

135. Constitution of 1885.

Kettleborough, 283.

DECLARATION OF RIGHTS

Sec. 5.   The free exercise and enjoyment of religious profession and worship shall forever be allowed in this State, and no person shall be rendered incompetent as a witness on account of his religious opinions; but the liberty of conscience hereby secured shall not be so construed as to justify licentiousness or practices subversive of, or inconsistent with, the peace or moral safety of the State or society.

Sec. 6.   No preference shall ever be given by law to any church, sect or mode of worship, and no money shall ever be taken from the public treasury directly or indirectly in aid of any church, sect or religious denomination, or in aid of any sectarian institution.

ARTICLE XII.

Sec. 4.   The State School Fund, the interest of which shall be exclusively applied to the support and maintenance of public free schools, shall be derived from the following sources: etc.

Sec. 5.   The principal of the State School Fund shall remain sacred and inviolate.

Sec. 12.   White and colored children shall not be taught in the same school, but impartial provision shall be made for both.

Sec. 13.   No law shall be enacted authorizing the diversion or the lending of any county or district school funds, or the appropriation of any part of the permanent or available school fund to any other than school purposes; nor shall the same, or any part thereof, be appropriated to or used for the support of any sectarian school.

ARTICLE XII.

Sec. 1.   [Militia]   . . . but no male citizen of whatever religious creed or opinion shall be exempt from military duty except upon such conditions as may be prescribed by law.

ARTICLE XIII.

Sec. 16.   The property of all corporations, except the property of a corporation which shall construct a ship or a barge canal across the peninsula of Florida, if the Legislature should so enact, whether heretofore or hereafter incorporated, shall be subject to taxation unless such property be held and used exclusively for religious, scientific, municipal, educational, literary or charitable purposes.

XXXIX.   SOUTH DAKOTA, 1889.

136.   Constitution of 1889.

Kettleborough, 1256.

From the Preamble

. . . grateful to Almighty God for our civil and religious liberty . . .

ARTICLE VI

Sec. 3.   The right to worship God according to the dictates of conscience shall never be infringed.   No person shall be denied any civil or political right, privilege or position on account of his religious opinions; but the liberty of conscience hereby secured shall not be so construed as to excuse licentiousness, the invasion of the rights of others, or justify practices inconsistent with the peace or safety of the State.
No person shall be compelled to attend or support any ministry or place of worship against his consent nor shall any preference be given by law to any religious establishment or mode of worship.   No money or property of the state shall be given or appropriated for the benefit of any sectarian or religious society or institution.

ARTICLE VIII.

Sec. 16.   No appropriation of money, lands, or other property or credits to aid any sectarian school shall ever be made by the state, or any county or municipality within the state, nor shall the state or any county or municipality within the state accept any grant, conveyance, gift or bequest of lands, money, or other property to be used for sectarian purposes, and no sectarian instruction shall be allowed in any school or institution aided or supported by the state.

ARTICLE XI.

Sec. 6. The Legislature shall by general law, exempt from taxation, property used exclusively for agricultural and horticultural societies, for school, religious, cemetery. . . .

ARTICLE XV.

Sec. 7. No person having conscientious scruples against bearing arms shall be compelled to do military duty in time of peace.

ARTICLE XXII.

First. That perfect toleration of religious sentiment shall be secured, and that no inhabitant of this state shall ever be molested in person or property on account of his or her mode of religious worship.

Fourth. That provision shall be made for the establishment and maintenance of systems of public schools, which shall be open to all the children of this State, and free from sectarian control.

XL.   NORTH DAKOTA, 1889

137.   Constitution of 1889.

Kettleborough 1021.

From the Preamble

. . . grateful to Almighty God for the blessings of civil and religious liberty.

ARTICLE I.

Sec. 4. The free exercise and enjoyment of religious profession and worship, without discrimination or preference, shall be forever guaranteed in this state, and no person shall be rendered incompetent to be a witness or a juror on account of his opinions on matters of religious belief; but the liberty of conscience hereby secured shall not be so construed as to excuse acts of licentiousness, or justify practices inconsistent with the peace or safety of this state.

ARTICLE II.

Sec. 69.   The Legislative Assembly shall not pass local or special laws in any of the following cases:

20.   Granting to any corporation, association or individual . . . immunity or franchise whatever.

29.   Exempting property from taxation.

ARTICLE VIII.

Sec. 147.   [Public schools] . . . [shall provide a] system of public schools which shall be open to all children of the state of North Dakota and free from sectarian control.

Sec. 152.   No money raised for the support of the public schools of the state shall be appropriated to or used for the support of any sectarian school.

ARTICLE XI.

Sec. 176.   And the legislative assembly shall by a general law exempt from taxation property used exclusively for school, religious, cemetery, etc. . . . .

ARTICLE XIII.

Sec. 188.   [Militia]   Persons whose religious tenets or conscientious scruples forbid them to bear arms shall not be compelled to do so in times of peace, but shall pay an equivalent in personal service.

ARTICLE XVI.

Sec. 203.   First.   Perfect toleration of religious sentiment shall be secured, and no inhabitant of this State shall ever be molested in person or property on account of his or her mode of religious worship.

XLI.   MONTANA, 1889.

138.   Constitution of 1889.
Kettleborough, 816.

From the Preamble.

. . . grateful to Almighty God for the blessings of liberty . . .

ARTICLE III.

Sec. 4.   The free exercise and enjoyment of religious profession and worship without discrimination, shall forever hereafter be guaranteed, and no person shall be denied any civil or political right or privilege on account of his opinions concerning religion, but the liberty and conscience hereby secured shall not be construed to dispense with oaths or affirmations, excuse acts of licentiousness, by bigamous or polygamous marriage, or otherwise, or justify practices inconsistent with the good order, peace or safety of the state, or opposed to the civil authority thereof, or of the United States.   No person shall be required to attend any place of worship or support any ministry, religious sect or denomination, against his consent; nor shall any preference be given by law to any religious denomination or mode of worship.

ARTICLE V.

Sec. 26.   The Legislative assembly shall not pass local or special laws in any of the following enumerated cases, that is to say: . . . [corporations] . . . any special or exclusive privilege, immunity or franchise whatever . . . exempting property from taxation. . . .

Sec. 35.   No appropriations shall be made for charitable, industrial, educational or benevolent purposes to any person, corporation or community not under the absolute control of the State, nor to any denominational or sectarian institution or association.

ARTICLE XI

Sec. 2.   The public school fund of the state shall consist of the proceeds of such lands as have heretofore been granted, or may hereafter be granted, to the state by the general government, known as school lands, and those granted in lieu of such; lands acquired by gift or grant from any person or corporation under grants of land or money made to the state from the gen-

eral government for general educational purposes or where no
other special purpose is indicated in such grant; all estates, or
distributive shares of estates that may escheat to the State; all
unclaimed shares and dividends of any corporation incorporated
under the laws of the State, and all other grants, gifts, devises
or bequests made to the State for general educational purposes.

Sec. 8.   Neither the Legislative Assembly, nor any county,
city, town, or school district, or other public corporation, shall
shall ever make, directly or indirectly, any appropriation, or pay
from any public fund or moneys whatever, or make any grant of
lands or other property in aid of any church, or for any sectarian purpose, or to aid in the support of any school, academy,
seminary, college, university, or other literary, scientific institution, controlled in whole or in part by any church, sect or
denomination whatever.

Sec. 9.   No religious or partisan test or qualification shall
ever be required of any person as a condition of admission into
any public educational institution of the state, either as teacher
or student; nor shall attendance be required at any religious
service whatever, nor shall any sectarian tenets be taught in any
public educational institution of the State, nor shall any person
be debarred admission to any of the collegiate departments of
the university on account of sex.

ARTICLE XII.

Sec. 2.   [Tax exemption] . . . for educational purposes,
places for actual religious worship . . . may be exempt from taxation.

XLII.   WASHINGTON, 1889.

139.   Constitution of 1889.
Kettleborough, 1441.

From the Preamble

. . . grateful to the Supreme Ruler of the Universe for our
liberties . . .

ARTICLE I.

Sec. 11.   Absolute freedom of conscience in all matters of
religious sentiment, belief, and worship, shall be guaranteed to

every individual, and no one shall be molested or be disturbed in person or property on account of religion; but the liberty of conscience hereby secured shall not be so construed as to excuse acts of licentiousness or justify practices inconsistent with the peace and safety of the state. No public money shall be appropriated for or applied to any religious worship, exercise or instruction, or support of any religious establishment. Provided, however, That this article shall not be so construed as to forbid the employment by the State of a chaplain for the State penitentiary, and for such of the State reformatories as in the discretion of the Legislature may seem justified. No religious qualification shall be required for any public office or employment, nor shall any person be incompetent as a witness or juror, in consequence of his opinion on matters of religion, nor be questioned in any court of justice touching his religious beliefs to affect the weight of his testimony.

ARTICLE IX.

Sec. 2. . . . But the entire revenue derived from the common school fund, and the state tax for common schools, shall be exclusively applied to the support of the common schools.

Sec. 4. All schools maintained or supported wholly or in part by the public funds shall be forever free from sectarian control or influence.

ARTICLE X.

Sec. 6. No person or persons, having conscientious scruples against bearing arms, shall be compelled to do militia duty in time of peace: Provided, Such person or persons shall pay an equivalent for such exemption.

ARTICLE XXVI.

Compact with the United States.

First, That perfect toleration of religious sentiment shall be secured, and that no inhabitant of this state shall ever be molested in person or property on account of his or her mode of religious worship.

Fourth, Provision shall be made for the establishment and

maintenance of systems of public schools free from sectarian control, which shall be open to all the children of said state.

XLIII.   IDAHO, 1890.

140.   Constitution of 1890.
Kettleborough, 351.

From the Preamble.

. . . grateful to Almighty God for our freedom . . .

ARTICLE I.

Sec. 4.   The exercise and enjoyment of religious faith and worship shall forever be guaranteed; and no person shall be denied any civil or political right, privilege or capacity, on account of his religious opinions; but the liberty of conscience hereby secured shall not be construed to dispense with oaths or affirmations, or excuse acts of licentiousness or justify polygamous or other pernicious practices, inconsistent with morality or the peace or safety of the state; nor to permit any person, organization or association to directly or indirectly aid or abet, counsel or advise any person to commit the crime of bigamy or polygamy, or any other crime.   No person shall be required to attend or support any ministry or place of worship, religious sect or denomination or to pay tithes, against his consent; nor shall any preference be given by law to any religious denomination or mode of worship.   Bigamy and polygamy are forever prohibited in the state, and the legislature shall provide by law for the punishment of such crimes.

ARTICLE III.

Sec. 19.   The Legislature shall not pass local or special laws in any of the following enumerated cases, that is to say: Exempting property from taxation.

ARTICLE VI.

Sec. 3.   [Suffrage]   No person is permitted to vote . . . who is a bigamist or polygamist, or is living in what is known as patriarchical, plural or celestial marriage, or in violation of any law of this state . . . or who in any manner teaches, advises, counsels, aids or encourages any person to enter into bigamy, polygamy, or such patriarchial, plural or celestial marriage, or to live in violation of any such law, or to commit any such crime, or who is a member of, or continues to the support, aid, or encouragement of, any order, organization, association, corporation, or society which teaches or advises that the laws of this state prescribing rules of civil conduct, are not the supreme laws of the state, . . .

ARTICLE VII.

Sec. 5. . . . That the Legislature may allow such exemptions from taxation from time to time as shall seem necessary and just, and all existing exemptions provided by the laws of the territory, shall continue until changed by the legislature of the state.

ARTICLE IX.

Sec. 5. Neither the Legislature nor any county, city, town, township, school district, or any other public corporation, shall ever make any appropriation or pay from any public fund or moneys whatever, anything in aid of any church or sectarian, or religious society, or for any sectarian or religious purpose, or to help support or sustain any school, academy, seminary, college, university, or other literary or scientific institution, controlled by any church, sectarian, or religious denomination whatsoever, nor shall any grant or donation of land, money, or other personal property ever be made by the state or any public corporation to any church or for any sectarian or religious purpose.

Sec. 6. No religious test or qualification shall ever be required of any person as a condition of admission into any public educational institution of the state, either as a teacher or student, and no teacher or student of any such institution shall ever be required to attend or participate in any religious service whatever. No sectarian or religious tenets or doctrines shall ever be taught in the public schools, nor shall any distinction or classification of pupils be made on account of race or color. No books, papers, tracts or documents of a political, sectarian, or denominational character shall be used or introduced in any school established under the provision of this article, nor shall any teacher or any district receive any of the public moneys in which the schools have not been taught in accordance with the provisions of this article.

ARTICLE XIV.

Sec. 1. . . . but no person having conscientious scruples against bearing arms shall be compelled to perform such duty in time of peace.

ARTICLE XXI.

Sec. 19. It is ordained by the state of Idaho that perfect toleration of religious sentiment shall be secured and no inhabitant shall ever be molested in person or property on account of mode of worship.

XLIV. WYOMING, 1890.

141. Constitution of 1890.
Kettleborough, 1524.

From the Preamble.

. . . grateful to Almighty God for our civil, political and religious liberty . . .

ARTICLE I.

Sec. 18. The free exercise and enjoyment of religious profession and worship without discrimination or preference shall be forever guaranteed in this State, and no person shall be rendered incompetent to hold any office of trust or profit, or to serve as a witness or juror, because of his opinion on any matter of religious belief whatever; but the liberty of conscience hereby secured shall not be so construed as to excuse acts of licentiousness or justify practices inconsistent with the peace or safety of the State.

Sec. 19. No money of the State shall ever be given or appropriated to any sectarian or religious society or institution.

Sec. 30. . . . Corporations being creatures of the state, endowed for the public good with a portion of its sovereign powers, must be subject to its control.

ARTICLE III.

Sec. 27. The Legislature shall not pass local or special laws in any of the following cases, that is to say: . . . granting to any corporation, association or individual, . . . any special or exclusive privilege, immunity or franchise whatever or amending existing charter for such purpose . . . relinquishing or extinguishing in whole or part, the indebtedness, liabilities or obligation of any corporation or person to this state or to any municipal corporation therein; exempting property from taxation . . .

Sec. 36. No appropriation shall be made for charitable, industrial, educational or benevolent purposes to any person, corporation or community not under the absolute control of the state, nor to any denominational or sectarian institution or association.

ARTICLE VII.

Sec. 8. . . . But no appropriation shall be made from said fund to any . . . Seminary, college or other institution of learning controlled by any church or sectarian organization or religious denomination whatsoever.

Sec. 12. No sectarian instruction, qualifications or tests shall be imposed, enacted, applied or in any manner tolerated in the schools of any grade or character controlled by the State, nor shall attendance be required at any religious service therein, nor shall any sectarian tenets or doctrines be taught or favored in any public school or institution that may be established under this constitution.

ARTICLE X.

Sec. 2. All powers and franchises of corporations are derived from the people and are granted by their agent, the government, for the public good and the general welfare, and the right and duty of the state to control and regulate them for these purposes is hereby declared.

ARTICLE XV.

Sec. 12. The property of the United States, the states, counties, cities, towns, school districts, municipal corporations and public libraries, lots with the buildings thereon used exclusively for religious worship, church parsonages, public cemeteries, shall be exempt from taxation, and such other property as the legislature may by general law provide.

ARTICLE XVI.

Sec. 6.   Neither the state, nor any county, city, township, school district, or any other political subdivision, shall loan or give its credit or make donations to or in aid of any individual, association or corporation. . . .

ARTICLE XVII.

Sec. 1.   [Militia]   . . . But all such citizens having scruples of conscience averse to bearing arms shall be excused therefrom upon such conditions as shall be prescribed by law.

Ordinances.

ARTICLE XXI.

Sec. 2.   Perfect toleration of religious sentiment shall be secured, and no inhabitant of this state shall ever be molested in person or property on account of his or her mode of religious worship.

Sec. 5.   The legislature shall make laws for the establishment and maintenance of systems of public schools which shall be open to all the children of the state and free from sectarian control.

XX.   MISSISSIPPI

142.   Constitution of 1890.

Kettleborough, 738.

ARTICLE III.

Sec. 18.   No religious test as qualification for office shall be required; and no preference shall be given by law to any religious sect, or mode of worship; but the free enjoyment of all religious sentiments and the different modes of worship shall be held sacred. The rights hereby secured shall not be construed to justify acts of licentiousness injurious to morals or dangerous to the peace and safety of the State, or to exclude the Holy Bible from use in any school of this State.

ARTICLE VIII.

Sec. 208.   No religious or other sect, or sects, shall ever control any part of the school or other educational funds of this State; nor shall any funds be appropriated toward the support of any sectarian school; or to any school that at the time of receiving the appropriation is not conducted as a free school.

ARTICLE XII.

And all persons offering to register shall take the following oath or affirmation: "I ——— do solemnly swear (or affirm) that I am twenty-one years old, (or I will be before the next election in this county) and that I will have resided in this State two years and ——— election district of ——— county one year next preceding the ensuing election (or if it be stated in the oath that the person proposing to register is a minister of the gospel in charge of an organized church, then it will be sufficient to aver therein two years residence in the State and six months in said election district), etc. . .

ARTICLE XIV.

Sec. 265.   No one who denies the existence of a Supreme Being shall hold any office in this State.

Sec. 269.   Every devise or bequest of lands, tenements or hereditaments, of any interest therein, of freehold, or less than freehold, either present or future, vested or contingent, or of any money directed to be raised by the sale thereof, contained in any last will and testament, codicil, or other testamentary writing in favor of any religious or ecclesiastical corporation, sole or aggregate, or any religious or ecclesiastical society, or to any religious denomination or association or persons, or to any person or body politic, in trust, either expressed or implied, secret or resulting, either for the use and benefit of such religious corporation, society, denomination, or association, or for the purpose of being given or appropriated to charitable uses or purposes, shall be null and void, and the heir-at-law shall take the same property so devised or bequeathed, as though no testamentary disposition had been made.

Sec. 270. Every legacy, gift or bequest, of money or personal property, or of any interest, benefit or use therein, either direct, implied or otherwise, contained in any last will and testament or codicil, in favor of any religious or ecclesiastical corporation, sole or aggregate, or any religious or ecclesiastical society, or to any religious denomination or association, either for its own use or benefit, or for the purpose of being given or appropriated to charitable uses, shall be null and void, and the distributees shall take the same as though no such testamentary disposition had been made.

XV.   KENTUCKY

143.   Constitution of 1891.

Kettleborough, 466.

Bill of Rights, Sec. 1.

Second.   The right of worshipping Almighty God according to the dictates of their consciences.

Fourth.   The right of freely communicating their thoughts and opinions.

Sixth.   The right of assembling together in a peaceable manner for their common good, and of applying to those invested with the power of government for redress of grievances or other proper purposes, by petition, address or remonstrance.

Sec. 5.   No preference shall ever be given by law to any religious sect, society or denomination, nor to any particular creed, mode of worship or system of ecclesiastical policy; nor shall any person be compelled to attend any place of worship, to contribute to the erection or maintenance of any such place, or to the salary, or support of any minister of religion; nor shall any man be compelled to send his child to any school to which he may be conscientiously opposed; and the civil rights, privileges or capacities of no person shall be taken away, or in any wise diminished or enlarged, on account of his belief or disbelief of any religious tenet, dogma or teaching. No human authority shall, in any case whatever, control or interfere with the rights of conscience.

Sec. 170. There shall be exempt from taxation public property used for public purposes; places actually used for religious worship, with the grounds attached thereto and used and appurtenant to the house of worship; . . . institutions of education not used or employed for gain by any person or corporation . . . all parsonages or residences owned by any religious society, and occupied as a home, and for no other purpose, by the minister of any religion, with not exceeding one-half acre of ground in towns and cities and two acres of ground in the country. . . .

Sec. 189. No portion of any fund or tax now existing, or that may hereafter be raised or levied for educational purposes, shall be appropriated to, or used, by or in aid of any church, sectarian, or denominational school.

Sec. 220. The General Assembly shall provide for maintaining an organized militia; and may exempt from military service persons having conscientious scruples against bearing arms; but such persons shall pay an equivalent for such exemption.

IX. NEW YORK.

144. Article IX. 4, 1894.

Sec. 4. Neither the state nor any subdivision thereof, shall use its property or credit or any public money, or authorize or permit either to be used, directly or indirectly, in aid or maintenance, other than for examination or inspection, of any school or institution of learning wholly or in part under the control or direction of any religious denomination, or in which any denominational tenet or doctrine is taught.

XII. DELAWARE.

145. Constitution of 1897.

Kettleborough, 253.

From the Preamble (corresponds to 1892)

Through Divine goodness, all men have by nature, the rights of worshipping and serving their Creator according to the dictates of their consciences. . . .

From Article I, Bill of Rights (as 1892)

Sec. 1.   Although it is the duty of all men frequently to assemble together for the public worship of God . . . yet no man shall or ought to be compelled to attend any religious worship, to contribute to the erection or support of any place of worship, or to the maintenance of any ministry, against his own free will and consent; and no power ought to be vested in or assumed by any magistrate that shall in any case interfere with, or control the rights of conscience, in the free exercise of religious worship, nor a preference given by law to any religious societies, denominations or modes of worship.

Sec. 2.   No religious test shall be required as a qualification to any office, or public trust, under this State.

ARTICLE VIII.

Sec. 1.   . . . But the General Assembly may by general laws exempt from taxation such property as in the opinion of the general assembly will best promote the public welfare.

ARTICLE IX.

Sec. 4.   The rights, privileges and immunities and estates of religious societies and corporate bodies, except as herein otherwise provided, shall remain as if the Constitution of this State had not been altered.

ARTICLE X.

Sec. 3.   No portion of any fund now existing, or which may hereafter be appropriated, or raised by tax, for educational purposes, shall be appropriated to, or used by, or in aid of any sectarian church or denominational school; provided, that all real or personal property used for school purposes, where the tuition is free, shall be exempt from taxation and assessment for public purposes.

Sec. 4.   No part of the principal or income of the Public School Fund now or hereafter existing, shall be used for any other purpose than the support of free public schools.

XLV.   UTAH, 1896.

146.   Constitution of 1895.
Kettleborough, 1352.

From the Preamble.
Grateful to Almighty God for life and liberty.

ARTICLE I.

Sec. 4.   The rights of conscience shall never be infringed. The State shall make no law respecting an establishment of religion or prohibiting the free exercise thereof; no religious test shall be required as a qualification for any office of public trust or for any vote at any election; nor shall any person be incompetent as a witness or juror on account of religious belief or the absence thereof.   There shall be no union of Church and State, nor shall any church dominate the state or interfere with its functions.   No public money or property shall be appropriated for or applied to any religious worship, exercise or instruction, or for the support of any ecclesiastical establishment.
No property qualification shall be required of any person to vote or hold office, except as provided in this Constitution.

ARTICLE III.

First.   Perfect toleration of religious sentiment is guaranteed.   No inhabitant of this State shall ever be molested in person or property on account of his or her mode of religious worship: but polygamous or plural marriages are forever prohibited.

ARTICLE VI.

Sec. 26.   The Legislature is prohibited from enacting any private or special laws in the following cases:
16.   Granting to any individual, association or corporation any privilege, immunity or franchise.
Sec. 27.   The Legislature shall have no power to release or extinguish in whole or in part, the indebtedness, liability or obligation of any corporation or person to the State . . .

ARTICLE X.

Sec. 1.   The Legislature shall provide for the establishment and maintenance of a uniform system of public schools, which shall be open to all children of the state and be free from sectarian control.

Sec. 12.   Neither religious nor partisan test or qualification shall be required of any person, as a condition of admission, as teacher or student into any public educational institution of the State.

Sec. 13.   Neither the Legislature nor any county, city, town, school district or other public corporation, shall make any appropriation to aid in the support of any school, seminary, college, university or other institution, controlled in whole, or in part, by any church, sect or denomination whatever.

ARTICLE XII.

Sec. 1.   Corporations may be formed under the general laws, but shall not be created by special acts.

ARTICLE XIII.

Sec. 3.   [Revenue and Taxation]

The Legislature shall provide by law a uniform and equal rate of assessment and taxation on all property in the State. . . . Provided that . . . lots with the buildings thereon used exclusively for either religious worship or charitable purposes . . . shall be exempt from taxation.

Sec. 10.   All corporations or persons in this State or doing business therein, shall be subject to taxation for State, County, School.

XXII.   ALABAMA.

147.   Article XIV, 263, 1901.

No money raised for the support of the public schools shall be appropriated to or used for the support of any sectarian or denominational school.

I.   VIRGINIA.

148.   Constitution of 1902.

Kettleborough, 1394.

Section 16 corresponds to 16 of 1776.
Section 58 corresponds to IV, 15 of 1850.
Section 59 corresponds to IV, 32 of 1776.

ARTICLE IV.

Sec. 67.   The General Assembly shall not make any appropriation of public funds, of personal property, or of real estate, to any church, or sectarian society, association, or instruction of any kind whatever; which is entirely or partly, directly or indirectly, controlled by any church or sectarian society . . .

ARTICLE IX.

Sec. 141.   No appropriation of public funds shall be made to any school or institution of learning not owned or exclusively controlled by the State or some political sub-division thereof; . . .

ARTICLE XIII.

Sec. 183.   (B)   Buildings, with land they actually occupy, and the furniture and furnishings therein lawfully owned and held by churches or religious bodies, and wholly and exclusively used for religious worship, or for the residence of the minister of such church or religious body, together with the additional adjacent land reasonably necessary for the convenient use of any such building.

(D)   Buildings with the land they actually occupy, and the furniture, furnishings, books and instruments therein to . . . and used by churches . . . seminaries . . . and also the buildings thereon used as residences by the officers or instructors of such educational institutions, and also the permanent endowment funds held by . . . such educational institutions directly or in trust . . . [shall be exempt].

Sec. 185.   Neither the credit of the State, nor of the county, city or town shall be directly or indirectly, under any device or pretence whatever, granted to or in aid of any person, association or corporation; nor shall the State, or any county, city, or town subscribe to or become interested in the stock or obligations of any company, association or corporation, for the purpose of aiding in the construction or maintenance of its work;

XLVI.   OKLAHOMA, 1907.

149.   Constitution of 1907.

Kettleborough, 1091.

From the Preamble

Invoking the guidance of Almighty God . . .

ARTICLE I.

Sec. 2. Perfect toleration of religious sentiment shall be secured, and no inhabitant of this state shall ever be molested in person or property on account of his or her mode of religious worship: and no religious test shall be required for the exercise of civil or political rights. Polygamous or plural marriages are forever prohibited.

Sec. 5. Provisions shall be made for the establishment and maintenance of a system of public schools, which shall be open to all children of the State and free from sectarian control.

ARTICLE II.

Sec. 5. No public money or property shall ever be appropriated, applied, donated, or used, directly or indirectly, for the use, benefit, or support of any sect, church, denomination, or system of religion, or for the use, benefit, or support of any priest, teacher, minister, or other religious teacher or dignitary, or sectarian institution as such.

ARTICLE V.

Sec. 50. The Legislature shall pass no law exempting any property within this state from taxation, except as otherwise provided in this constitution.

Sec. 51. The Legislature shall pass no law granting to any association, corporation, or individual any exclusive rights, privileges, or immunities within this State.

ARTICLE IX.

Sec. 13. No railroad or transportation company or transmission company shall, directly or indirectly, issue or give any free frank or free ticket, free pass or other free transportation for any use, within this State except to . . . *ministers of religion.*

ARTICLE X.

Sec. 6. All property used for free public libraries, free

museums, public cemeteries, property used exclusively for schools, colleges, and all property used exclusively for religious and charitable purposes . . . shall be exempt from taxation unless otherwise provided by law.

ARTICLE XI.

Sec. 5. . . . and no part of the proceeds arising from the sale or disposal of any lands granted for educational purposes, or the income or rentals thereof, shall be used for the support of any religious or sectarian school, college or university . . .

XXVI. MICHIGAN

150. Constitution of 1908.

Kettleborough, 685.

ARTICLE II.

Sec. 3. Every person shall be at liberty to worship God according to the dictates of his own conscience. No person shall be compelled to attend, or, against his consent, to contribute to the erection or support of any place of religious worship, or to pay tithes, taxes or other rates for the support of any minister of the Gospel or teacher of religion. No money shall be appropriated or drawn from the treasury for the benefit of any religious sect or society, theological or religious seminary; nor shall property belonging to the state be appropriated for any such purpose.
The civil and political rights, privileges and capacities of no person shall be diminished or enlarged on account of his religious belief.

ARTICLE XII.

Sec. 3. No corporation shall be created for a longer period than thirty years, except for municipal, railroad, insurance, canal or cemetery purposes, or corporations organized without any capital stock for religious, benevolent, social or fraternal purposes; but the Legislature may provide by general laws, applicable to any corporations, for one or more extensions of the term of such corporations.

ARTICLE XV.

Sec. 1. [Militia] . . .; but all such citizens of any religious denomination, who, from scruples of conscience, may be averse to bearing arms, shall be excused therefrom upon such conditions as may be prescribed by law.

XLVII. NEW MEXICO, 1912.

151. Constitution of 1912.

Kettleborough, 937.

From the Preamble

. . . grateful to Almighty God for the blessings of liberty. . .

ARTICLE II.

Sec. 5. The rights, privileges, and immunities, civil, political, and religious guaranteed to the people of New Mexico, by the Treaty of Guadalupe Hidalgo shall be preserved inviolate.

Sec. 11. Every man shall be free to worship God according to the dictates of his own conscience, and no person shall ever be molested or denied any civil or political right or privilege on account of his religious opinion or mode of religious worship. No person shall be required to attend any place of worship or support any religious sect or denomination; nor shall any preference be given by law to any religious denomination or mode of worship.

ARTICLE IV.

Sec. 24. The Legislature shall not pass local or special laws in any of the following cases: . . . granting to any corporation, association . . . any special or exclusive privilege, immunity or franchise . . . exempting property from taxation.

Sec. 26. The Legislature shall not grant to any corporation or person any rights, franchises, privileges, immunities, or exemptions, which shall not, upon the same terms, and under like conditions, inure equally to all persons or corporations . . .

Sec. 31. No appropriation shall be made for charitable, educational, or other benevolent purposes to any person, corporation, association, institution or community not under the absolute control of the state . . .

ARTICLE VII.

Sec. 3. The right of any citizen of the State to vote, hold office, or sit in upon juries, shall never be restricted, abridged, or impaired on account of religion, race, language, color . . .

ARTICLE VIII (as amended 1914)

Sec. 7. . . . all church property, all property used for educational or charitable purposes . . . shall be exempt from taxation.

ARTICLE IX.

Sec. 14. Neither the State, nor any county, school district, or municipality except as otherwise provided in this constitution, shall directly or indirectly lend or pledge its credit, or make any donation to or in aid of any person, association or public or private corporation, or in aid of any private enterprise . . .

ARTICLE XI.

Sec. 13. The legislature shall provide for the organization of corporations by general law.

ARTICLE XII

Sec. 3. . . . And no part of the proceeds arising from the sale or disposal of any lands granted to the State by Congress, or any other funds appropriated, levied, or collected for educational purposes, shall be used for the support of any sectarian, denominational, or private school, college, or university.

Sec. 9. No religious test shall ever be required as a condition of admission into the public schools or any educational institution of the state, either as a teacher or student, and no teacher or student of such school or institution shall ever be required to attend or participate in any religious service whatsoever.

ARTICLE XXI.

Sec. 1. Perfect toleration of religious sentiment shall be

secured, and no inhabitant of this State shall ever be molested in person or property on account of his or her mode of religious worship. Polygamous or plural marriages, polygamous cohabitation, ... are forever prohibited.

Sec. 4. Provision shall be made for the establishment and maintenance of a system of public schools which shall be open to all children of the state and free from sectarian control, and said schools shall always be conducted in English.

XLVIII.   ARIZONA, 1912.

152.   Constitution of 1912.

Kettleborough, 55.

From the Preamble.

... grateful to Almighty God for our liberties ...

ARTICLE II.

Sec. 7. The mode of administering an oath, or affirmation, shall be such as shall be most consistent with the binding upon the conscience of the person to whom such oath, or affirmation, may be administered.

Sec. 12. The liberty of conscience secured by the provisions of this Constitution shall not be construed as to excuse acts of licentiousness, or justify practices inconsistent with the peace and safety of the State. No public money or property shall be appropriated for or applied to any religious worship, exercise, or instruction, or to the support of any religious establishment. No religious qualification shall be required for any public office or employment, nor shall any person be incompetent as a witness or juror in consequence of his opinions on matters of religion, nor be questioned touching his religious belief in any court of justice to affect the weight of his testimony.

ARTICLE IX.

Sec. 2. There shall be exempted from taxation ... property of educational, charitable, and religious associations, or institutions not used or held for profit may be exempted from taxation by law.

Sec. 10. No tax shall be laid or appropriation of public

money made in aid of any church, or private or sectarian school, or in any public service corporation.

ARTICLE XI.

Sec. 7. No sectarian instruction shall be imparted in any school or State educational institution that may be established under this Constitution, and no religious or political test or qualification shall ever be required as a condition of admission into any public educational institution of the State, as student, teacher, or pupil; but the liberty of conscience hereby secured shall not be construed as to justify practices or conduct inconsistent with the good order, peace, morality, or safety of the State, or with the rights of others.

ARTICLE XX.

Sec. 1. Perfect toleration of religious sentiment shall be secured to every inhabitant of this State, and no inhabitant of this State shall ever be molested in person or property on account of his or her mode of religious worship, or lack of the same.

Sec. 7. Provisions shall be made by law for the establishment and maintenance of a system of public schools which shall be open to all children of the State and be free from sectarian control, and said school shall always be conducted in English.

XVIII LOUISIANA

153. Constitution of 1913.

Kettleborough, 501.

ARTICLE 4

Every person has the natural right to worship God, according to the dictates of his conscience, and no law shall be passed respecting an establishment of religion.

ARTICLE 48

The General Assembly shall not pass any local or special law on the following subjects:

Granting to any corporation, association, or individual any special or exclusive right, privilege or immunity.

Exempting property from taxation.

ARTICLE 53.

No money shall ever be taken from the public treasury, directly or indirectly, in aid of any church, sect or denomination of religion, or in aid of any priest, preacher, minister or teacher thereof, as such, and no preference shall ever be given to, nor any discrimination made against, any church, sect, or creed of religion, or any form of religious faith or worship, nor shall any appropriation be made for private, charitable or benevolent purposes to any person or community; provided, this shall not apply to the Louisiana Hospital for the Insane . . .

ARTICLE 229.

The General Assembly may levy a license tax and in such case shall graduate the amount of such tax to be collected from persons pursuing the several trades, professions, vocations, and callings. All persons, associations of persons and corporations pursuing any trade, profession, business or calling may be rendered liable to such tax, except clerks, laborers, clergymen. . . .

ARTICLE 230.

The following shall be exempt from taxation, and no other, viz.: All public property, places of religious worship, or burial, the rectories and parsonages of churches and grounds thereunto appurtenant, used exclusively as residences for the ministers in charge of such churches,

ARTICLE 235.

The Legislature shall have power to levy, solely for the support of the public schools, a tax upon all inheritances, legacies, and donations . . . provided, bequests to educational, religious, or charitable institutions shall be exempt from this tax.

ARTICLE 253

No funds raised for the support of the public schools of the

State shall be appropriated to or used for the support of any private or sectarian schools.

ARTICLE 300

The General Assembly may exempt from military service those who belong to religious societies whose tenets forbid them to bear arms; provided, a money equivalent for those services shall be exacted.

II. MASSACHUSETTS

154. Article XLVI, Sec. 2, 1917:

Public money not to be expended to aid educational charitable, religious or other institutions not wholly under public ownership and control . . .

F.

Since the United States Supreme Court Decision in the Louisiana Text-book case, A. D. 1930.

155. *The Hughes decision of April 28, 1930, and subsequent applications.*

Chief Justice Hughes in the Louisiana text-book case:

One may scan the acts in vain to ascertain where any money is appropriated for the purchase of the school books for the use of any church, private, sectarian or even public school. The appropriations were made for the specific purpose of purchasing school books for the use of the school children of the State, free of cost to them. It was for their benefit and the resulting benefit to the State that the appropriations were made.

True, these children attend some school, public or private, the latter, sectarian or nonsectarian, and that the books are to be furnished them for their use, free of cost, whichever they attend. The schools, however, are not the beneficiaries of these appropriations. They obtain nothing from them, nor are they relieved of a single obligation because of them. The school children and the State alone are the beneficiaries. It is also true that the sectarian schools, which some of the children attend, instruct their pupils in religion and books are used for that purpose, *but one may search diligently the acts, though without result, in an effort to find anything to the effect that it is the purpose of the use of such books.*

What the statutes contemplate is that the same books that are furnished children attending public schools shall be furnished children attending private schools. This is the only practical way of interpreting and executing the statutes, and this is what the State Board of Education is doing. *Among these books, naturally, none is to be expected adapted to religious instruction.* The decision was rendered April 28, 1930, 281 U. S. 370.

The Report of the President's Advisory Committee on Education, February 1938, included:

Consideration should be given, however, to the fact that large numbers of children receive instruction in nonpublic schools, and that the maintenance of schools under nonpublic auspices results in a significant reduction in public expense.

140

Many of the services of public schools should be available to children regardless of whether they are enrolled in public schools for instruction. It is therefore recommended that such portions of the general aid as may be allocated in the joint plans to the purchase of reading materials, transportation, and scholarships be made available so far as Federal legislation is concerned for the benefit of pupils both in public and in nonpublic schools. The Committee also recommends that local public schools receiving Federal aid be authorized to make their health and welfare services available to pupils in nonpublic schools. The conditions under which health and welfare services and aid for reading materials, transportation, and scholarships may be made available for pupils in privately controlled schools should be determined by the States, or by the local school jurisdiction receiving the grants if the States so determine. [Report of Committee, pp. 53-54.]

The New York Court of Appeals in June 1938 declared a law providing for transportation of parochial school children on a basis equivalent to that on which it is provided for public school children unconstitutional. But Chief Judge Crane in a dissenting opinion held:

The Statute in question does not have the effect of giving public money, property or credit in aid or maintenance of religious schools. The aid is given to the pupils who are legally attending such schools, to assist them to spend the required time in attendance upon instruction (278 N. Y. 200)

The Constitutional Amendments proposed by the New York State Constitutional Convention, 1938, include:

Article I.   Bill of Rights.

4.   To insure that no persons shall be denied the equal protection of the laws of the State or any subdivision thereof, or be subjected to any discrimination in his civil rights because of race, color, creed or religion, by any other person, firm, corporation or institution or by the State or any agency or subdivision of the State.

Article XI.   Education.

3.   To except from the present prohibition against the State or any subdivision using its property or credit in aid, other than for examination or inspection, of any institution of learn-

ing wholly or partly under control or direction of any religious denomination or in which any religious doctrine is taught, the transportation of children to and from any school or institution of learning, if so provided by the legislature.

Amendment 8.

(1) the money of the State shall not be given or loaned to or in aid of any private corporation or association or private undertaking, but that such provisions shall not apply to any fund or property now held or which may hereafter be held by the State for educational purposes, (2) subject to the limitations on indebtedness and taxation, nothing in the Constitution shall prevent the legislature from providing for the aid, care and support of the needy directly or through subdivision of the State, or for the protection by insurance or otherwise, against the hazards of unemployment, sickness and old age, or for the education and support of the blind, the deaf, the dumb, the physically handicapped and juvenile delinquents, as it may deem proper. or for health and welfare services for all children, either directly or through subdivisions of the State, including school districts, or for the aid, care and support of neglected and dependent children and of the needy sick, through agencies and institutions authorized by the state board of social welfare or other state department having the power of inspection thereof, by payments made on a percapita basis directly or through the subdivisions of the State, and that the enumeration of legislative powers in this item (2) shall not be taken to diminish any power of the legislature hitherto existing.

INDEX

[References are to Sections]